ACADEMIC CONNECTIONS 1

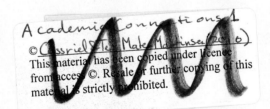

ACADEMIC CONNECTIONS 1

BETSY CASSRIEL

MARIT TER-MATE MARTINSEN

Academic Connections 1

Pearson Education, 10 Bank Street, White Plains, NY 10606

Staff credits: The people who made up the *Academic Connections 1* team, representing editorial, production, design, and manufacturing, are Pietro Alongi, Andrew Blasky, Aerin Csigay, Christine Edmonds, Ann France, Shelley Gazes, Gosia Jaros-White, Lise Minovitz, Sherry Preiss, Karen Quinn, Robert Ruvo, and Debbie Sistino.

ETS staff credits: The ETS people who made up the *Academic Connections* team, representing research, test design and scoring, item development, statistical analysis, and literature reviews, are Matthew Chametzky, Terry Cryan, Phil Everson, Elizabeth Jenner, Kate Kazin, Dawn Leusner, Brad Moulder, Jan Plante, Jonathon Schmidt, and Jody Stern.

Project editors: John Beaumont, Mykan White
Cover art: Art on File/Corbis
Text composition: Kirchoff/Wohlberg, Inc.
Text font: 11/13 Times Roman
Reviewers: See page xxvi

Library of Congress Cataloging-in-Publication Data

Academic connections. -- 1st ed.
   p. cm.
  ISBN 0-13-233843-2 (Level 1) -- ISBN 0-13-233844-0 (Level 2) -- ISBN 0-13-233845-9 (Level 3) -- ISBN 0-13-233841-6 (Level 4) 1. English language--Rhetoric--Problems, exercises, etc. 2. Report writing--Problems, exercises, etc. 3. Listening--Problems, exercises, etc. 4. Reading comprehension--Problems, exercises, etc. 5. College readers. I. Cassriel, Betsy. II. Martisen, Marit ter-Mate III. Hill, David, 1937 Oct. 15- IV. Williams, Julia
  PE1408.A223 2010
  428.0071'1--dc22

                                        2009017781

ISBN-10: 0-13-233843-2
ISBN-13: 978-0-13-233843-1

Printed in the United States of America
1 2 3 4 5 6 7 8 9 10—CRK—14 13 12 11 10 09

We would like to dedicate this book to our fathers.

To pa, who continues to inspire me.
M.M.

To my dad, who was proud of me.
B.C.

CONTENTS

WELCOME TO **ACADEMIC CONNECTIONS**

Academic Connections is a four-level, integrated skills course designed for students **preparing for academic study** as well as for **standardized tests**. A systematic, building-block approach helps students develop and sharpen their language skills as well as their academic and test-taking abilities.

The ACADEMIC CONNECTIONS Series Is

INTEGRATED

- *Academic Connections* **integrates** all four language skills—reading, listening, writing, and speaking.
- *Academic Connections* teaches students **how to integrate skills** and **content** in real-world academic contexts.
- **Integration of various media** empowers students and instills confidence.

ACADEMIC

- Academic skills and content prepare students for **success in the classroom** and on **standardized tests**.
- Explicit, **step-by-step skill development** leads to student mastery. With careful instruction and engaging practice tasks, students learn how to **organize information**, **make connections**, and **think critically**.
- Key **academic skills** are introduced, reinforced, and expanded in all four levels to facilitate acquisition.

AUTHENTIC

- **High-interest** and **intellectually stimulating authentic material** familiarizes students with content they will encounter in academic classes. Readings and lectures are excerpted or adapted from textbooks, academic journals, and other academic sources.

- Course content covers five **academic content areas**: Social Science, Life Science, Physical Science, Business and Marketing, and Arts and Literature.

- **Authentic tasks**, including listening to lectures, note-taking, participating in debates, preparing oral and written reports, and writing essays, prepare students for the demands of the content class.

ASSESSMENT-BASED

Academic Connections provides a **variety of assessments** that result in more effective student practice opportunities based upon individual needs:

- A *placement* test situates students in the appropriate level.
- *Pre-course* and *post-course* tests allow teachers to target instruction and measure achievement.
- *Multi-unit* tests track individual and class progress.
- *Formative assessments* monitor student skill mastery, allowing teachers to assign individualized exercises focused on the specific learning needs of the class.

RESEARCH-BASED

- *Academic Connections* was developed in cooperation with the **Educational Testing Service (ETS)**, creators of the TOEFL® test. The blend of curriculum and assessment is based on research that shows when English language learners are provided with authentic tasks, individualized and target practice opportunities, and timely feedback, they are better able to develop and integrate their reading, writing, speaking, and listening skills.

PERSONALIZED

PEARSON LONGMAN
myacademicconnectionslab

MyAcademicConnectionsLab, an easy-to-use **online** learning and assessment program, is an integral part of the *Academic Connections* series.

MyAcademicConnectionsLab offers:

- **Unlimited access** to reading and listening selections with online glossary support.
- **Original activities** that support the *Academic Connections* program. These include activities that build academic skills and vocabulary.
- **Focused test preparation** to help students succeed academically and on international exams. Regular **formative** and **summative assessments**, developed by ETS experts, provide evidence of student learning and progress.
- **Individualized instruction**, **instant feedback**, and **personalized study** plans help students improve results.
- **Time-saving tools** include a **flexible gradebook** and **authoring features** that give teachers **control of content** and help them **track student progress**.

THE **ACADEMIC CONNECTIONS** UNIT

UNIT OPENER

Each unit in the *Academic Connections* series begins with a captivating opener that outlines the unit's content, academic skills, and requirements. The outline mirrors an authentic academic syllabus and conveys the unit's academic purpose.

The content in *Academic Connections* is organized around five academic disciplines: Social Sciences, Life Sciences, Physical Sciences, Business and Marketing, and Arts and Literature.

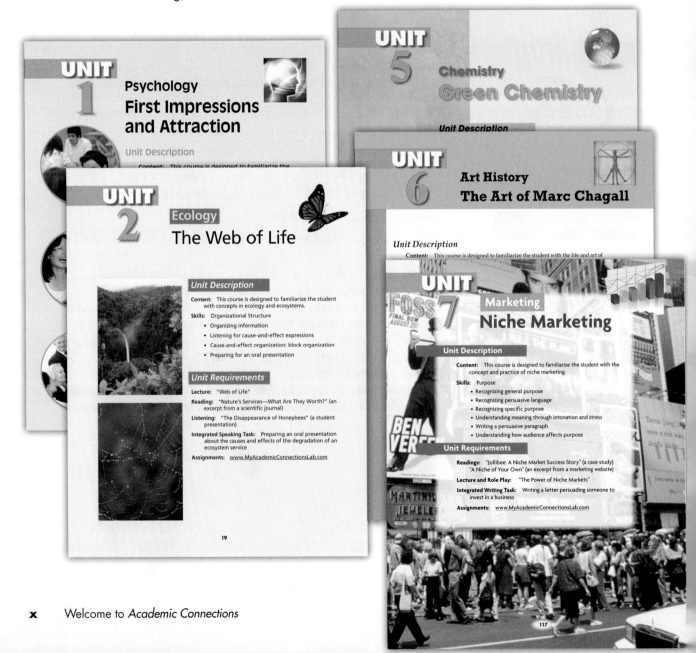

1 Preview

This section introduces students to the theme of the unit.

Previewing the Academic Content gives an overview of the topic, engages students in it, and exposes them to key words they will need in order to proceed.

---

1 Preview

For online assignments, go to

myacademicconnectionslab

Previewing the Academic Content

The late nineteenth and early twentieth centuries were a time of great change in art. Before this time, artists tried to make paintings look realistic. The new artists, like Pablo Picasso, used an abstract style to show ideas about people and objects without showing how they looked in reality. They shocked the art world with their modern techniques. In one such kind of art—cubism—images were made up of shapes like circles and squares or patterns seen from different views. These objects and people did not look real. Russian artist Marc Chagall was greatly influenced by the abstract work and artists of his time, but Chagall is famous for his own style of modern art. In this unit, you will explore the life and work of Marc Chagall.

1. Many artists paint self-portraits, or pictures of themselves. Study the three self-portraits. They are examples of three different styles of art. Number the paintings from 1 (most realistic) to 3 (most abstract). Then work in small groups to answer the questions.

Vincent Van Gogh.
Self-Portrait with Pipe and Straw Hat. 1888. Oil on canvas.

Marc Chagall.
Self-Portrait with Seven Fingers. 1913.
Oil on canvas.

Peter Paul Rubens.
Self-Portrait. 1638–1640.
Oil on canvas.

1. What makes the paintings realistic? What makes them abstract?
2. Which paintings do you like? Which ones do you not like? Why?

2. Like Chagall, many artists in the early twentieth century were influenced by the new abstract style in art. Lyubov Popova was one such artist. Work with a partner. Compare Popova's painting Lady with the Guitar to Chagall's I and the Village on the next page. Then discuss the questions with a partner. Use the key words in your discussion.

In this unit, you will practice synthesizing information in readings and lectures. You will also practice synthesizing information in your own writing.

Previewing the Academic Skills Focus

Synthesizing Information

In academic classes, you will often need to use different sources to find information about a topic. The sources may include written texts, lectures, discussions, graphs or charts, the Internet, or even your own knowledge about the world. Using many different sources will help you understand the topic better. When you connect information from different sources and use it to express your own ideas, you **synthesize** the information.

To synthesize information, you might connect ideas in one text to:
- other ideas in the same text (within text)
- ideas in other texts or lectures (text to text)
- your experience or personal knowledge (text to self)
- commonly known facts or events (text to world)

1. Look at the graph and read the excerpt from an article.

Average World Temperatures and Fossil Fuel¹ Use

In the past 50 years, Earth's temperatures have been increasing quickly. Richard Wool of the University of Delaware writes, "We have a very, very serious problem . . . called global warming." (2007) Global warming, the increase in Earth's temperatures, may have serious effects on our planet, including dangerous weather and storms. Many experts agree that pollution from burning fossil fuels like petroleum can cause global warming. John Warner of the University of Massachusetts in Lowell, says people who make chemicals need to think about the consequences. They should take steps to make products cleaner and safer to use.

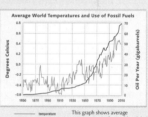

This graph shows average temperatures in the world and the use of fossil fuels.

† *fossil fuels n fuels, such as gas and oil, that formed from plants and animals that lived millions of years ago*

Previewing the Academic Skills Focus gives an overview of the academic skill for the unit. The material activates students' awareness of the skill and then prompts them to use it on a global level.

2 and 3
Building Academic Reading and Listening Skills

Sections 2 and 3 focus on academic reading and listening skills. First, students read a text or listen to a lecture on a topic related to the unit's academic discipline. They acquire reading and listening skills through careful instruction and engaging practice tasks.

Every unit includes both reading and listening.

Before You Read/Listen introduces students to the topic of the selection with pre-reading or pre-listening activities. The activities may include discussions that activate students' prior knowledge of the topic; they may also include vocabulary or brief academic skill practice.

MyAcademicConnectionsLab icons remind students to complete their online assignments.

2
Building Academic Reading Skills

In this section, you will practice distinguishing between facts and opinions.
For online assignments, go to
myacademicconnectionslab

Key Words

dreamlike *adj* as if happening in a dream
fantasy *n* an experience or situation that you imagine but is not real; **fantastic** *adj*
independent *adj* not controlled by other people
inspire *v* to make someone want to do something
modernism *n* a style of art and building that was especially popular from the 1940s to the 1960s, in which artists used simple shapes; **modernistic** *adj*
theme *n* the main idea or subject in a book, movie, painting, speech, etc.
universal *adj* true or right in every situation

Before You Read

1. Read the timeline of Marc Chagall's life.

WORLD EVENTS			MARC CHAGALL'S LIFE
		1887	Chagall is born into a large Jewish family in Vitebsk, Russia.
Pablo Picasso and Georges Braque begin to develop the cubist style of art.	1906–1908	1907–1910	Chagall studies many styles of art in St. Petersburg, Russia. He is in jail for a short time because he does not have a permit[1] to live there. At this time, Jews need a permit to live in St. Petersburg.
		1910–1914	Chagall lives in Paris, France. Cubist and modernist artists inspire him, but he develops his own independent style. Chagall paints some of his most famous work, showing many universal themes.
World War I begins.	1914	1914	Chagall returns to Russia.
		1915	Chagall marries Bella Rosenfeld, who is the subject of many of his paintings.
		1916	Chagall's daughter Ida is born.
The Russian Revolution happens.	1917		
World War I ends.	1918		
		1923	Chagall returns to Paris with his wife and daughter.
World War II begins.	1939		Chagall lives in Paris. Nazis destroy much of his art.
The Nazis occupy[2] Europe and persecute[3] Jews.	1941		Chagall lives in the United States.
		1944	Bella dies.
World War II ends.	1945		
		1948	Chagall moves from the United States back to Paris, France.
		1952	Chagall marries Valentina Brodsky.
		1958	Chagall begins working on larger projects, such as colorful glass windows in public and religious buildings.
		1985	Chagall dies in Saint-Paul de Vence, France.

[1] **permit** *n* an official written statement giving a person the right to do something
[2] **occupy** *v* to enter a place in a large group and keep control of it, especially by military force
[3] **persecute** *v* to treat someone badly because of his or her religious or political beliefs

Unit 6 ■ The Art of Marc Chagall **103**

3
Building Academic Listening Skills

In this section, you will practice listening for and taking notes on the main ideas and details of a lecture.
For online assignments, go to
myacademicconnectionslab

Key Words

element *n* one part of a whole
physical *adj* relating to the body, not the mind or soul
quality *n* a part of someone's personality
romantic *adj* showing strong feelings of love
session *n* a meeting for a particular purpose
similar *adj* almost the same, but not exactly the same; **similarity** *n*

Before You Listen

Peter M. Todd (2007), a psychologist from Indiana University, studied speed dating to learn more about elements of attraction. At speed-dating sessions, people try to find a romantic partner—someone to have a loving relationship with. Two people meet and talk for a very short time. After three to 10 minutes, they move to meet another person and so on. After that, they decide which men or women they want to see again. In his study, Todd wanted to find out two things:

■ what qualities people said they wanted in a romantic partner

■ what qualities really attracted people to each other during the speed-dating session

Todd studied how important certain qualities were to participants:

■ similarity to themselves
■ physical beauty
■ having a good job
■ the belief that family is important

Todd, P.M. et al. (2007). Different cognitive processes underlie human mate choices and mate preferences. *PNAS, 104(38),* 15011–15016.

1. What qualities are most important to you in a romantic partner? Number the qualities in order of importance from 1 to 4. Number 1 is the most important, and number 4 is the least important.

_____ 1. a person who is similar to me
_____ 2. a person with physical beauty
_____ 3. a person with a good job
_____ 4. a person who thinks family is very important

2. Work as a class to complete the chart. Write the number of men and women in your class who wrote 1 for each item in Exercise 1. Then add up the total. Do most people in your class agree on what is most important in a romantic partner? Do men and women agree?

Quality	Men	Women	Total
similar to me			
physical beauty			
good job			
family is very important			

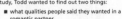 Unit 1 ■ First Impressions and Attraction **9**

---

(3) *limited / expanding* market. For example, when it introduced iTunes, it made a large (4) *consultant / profit* because other businesses were not serving the needs of customers who wanted to buy music online. After its success with iTunes, Apple (5) *expanded / consulted* its profit with other tools, such as the iPhone.

3. *You will listen to a lecture and role play. The title of the lecture is The Power of Niche Marketing. Based on the title, what do you predict is the general purpose of the lesson?*

Global Listening

1. 🎧 *Listen to the lecture and role play. Take notes on the main ideas.*

2. *Read the statements. Decide if they are true or false. Write **T** (true) or **F** (false). Use your notes. Then check your answers with a partner.*

_____ 1. The goal of niche marketing is to serve a large part of the market that most competitors don't serve.

_____ 2. Before expanding, businesses should become successful in a market niche.

_____ 3. When a business knows who has the biggest need for its product, it can fill these customers' needs better.

_____ 4. If a small business tries to attract a large market right away, it will probably run out of customers.

Recognizing Specific Purpose

A speaker or writer's **specific purpose** is his or her reason for making a specific statement or including certain information. Much of the specific information a speaker or writer includes will support the general purpose, so recognizing specific purpose can help you understand important ideas.

These are some common specific purposes:

• to give an example or to illustrate a point
• to show agreement or disagreement
• to request information
• to emphasize or show the importance of a point

A specific purpose may be stated directly. If it is not, you can ask these questions to recognize it:

• Why is the speaker (or writer) making this statement or including this information?
• What does the speaker (or writer) want the audience (the listeners or readers) to do?

Global Reading/Listening presents a selection that is adapted or excerpted from higher education textbooks or other academic sources. Comprehension and critical thinking activities lead students to an understanding of the selection on a global level. Students are also introduced to an academic skill that they practice by completing engaging tasks.

---

2. *Compare answers on page 41 with a partner's. Explain how the ideas you checked are related to the main idea.*

3. *Discuss the questions with your partner.*

1. Has stress ever caused you to do poorly at your work? Explain.
2. Has stress ever helped you (or someone you know) to do good work? Explain.
3. Has stress ever caused you (or someone you know) any health problems? Explain.

Global Reading

1. *Look at the pictures. Discuss the questions in small groups.*

1. What causes stress for the people in the pictures?
2. How is stress different for each person? Explain.

2. *Read the textbook excerpt. Take notes on the main ideas.*

Understanding Stress

1 Stress—the way a person responds to changes and difficult situations—is a common experience that people all over the world share (Blonna, 2005). In fact, most people have stressful experiences every day. However, research shows that people experience more stress today than they did in the past. Forty-eight percent of people in the United States report that they feel more stressed today than they did five years ago.[1] In addition, most doctor visits in the world (three out of five) happen because of problems related to stress.[2] Scientists and health workers are interested in

[1] APA survey, 2007
[2] Foundation for Integrated Research in Mental Health, 2007

In **Focused Reading/Listening**, students begin to explore the complexities of the selection. Comprehension, critical thinking, and/or inference activities in this section test students' detailed understanding of the text and lecture. This section might introduce another academic skill related to reading/listening and offer practice of the skill.

At the end of Sections 2 and 3, students are prompted to take an online test on **MyAcademicConnectionsLab**. These section tests (Checkpoints) monitor student progress and allow the teacher to assign individualized exercises focused on students' specific needs.

---

4. *Discuss your answers to Exercise 3 with the class. Did the same clues help you to recognize the specific purposes?*

Focused Listening

1. 🎧 *Listen to the lecture again. Complete the statements with the words from the box.*

buyers	Jollibee	large	limited	need	successful

1. Big companies may not serve a certain part of the market because it is not _____ enough for them to make a profit.

2. Many small businesses want to serve all customers even when they have a _____ amount of money.

3. Small business owners sometimes fear that if they focus on only one group of _____, they won't make enough of a profit.

4. A small business owner should always find out who has the biggest _____ for his or her product.

5. _____ is an example of a business that started small and grew bigger after becoming _____.

Understanding Meaning through Intonation and Stress

To express ideas clearly, speakers often use intonation and stress to give clues about their meaning.

Intonation is the rising ↑ and falling ↓ of your voice. Speakers can use intonation to show the meaning of a word or statement. Intonation often rises when someone is happy, excited, asking a question, or joking in a positive way. Intonation often falls when someone is upset, serious, or joking in a negative way.

🎧 Examples:
Twenty-five dollars for a meal! ↑ (Meaning: The meal is probably great and doesn't cost a lot.)
Twenty-five dollars for a meal! ↓ (Meaning: The meal costs too much.)

Stress is putting extra emphasis on certain words—for example, by saying them more loudly or slowly. A statement can have different meanings depending on which word is stressed.

🎧 Examples:
We saw a <u>funny</u> advertisement. (The ad wasn't sad or serious.)
We <u>saw</u> a funny advertisement. (We didn't hear the ad. We saw it.)
<u>We</u> saw a funny advertisement. (We saw the ad, but you didn't.)

---

1. *Circle the question words in the Questions column of the chart. Then scan the reading on page 6 to answer the questions.*

Questions	Answers
1. How long does it take to make a first impression?	a few seconds
2. What are four things people notice when they first meet someone?	
3. When did Snyder and Swan complete their study?	
4. Who studied people's predictions about relationships?	
5. How many first-year college students were in Sunnafrank's study?	

2. *Discuss the questions in small groups.*

1. Describe a recent first impression you had of someone. What do you predict about your relationship with this person?

2. Have you ever experienced the primacy effect? Have you experienced self-fulfilling prophecy? If so, describe what happened.

3. Many studies show that students do better in school when teachers expect them to be good students. Why do you think it is important for teachers, parents, and administrators to understand the idea of self-fulfilling prophecy?

Checkpoint 1 myacademicconnectionslab

4
Building Academic Writing/ Speaking Skills

This section emphasizes development of productive skills for writing or speaking. It presents language and academic skills needed for the integrated task. Students also read or listen to another selection that expands on or otherwise complements the earlier selections.

Each unit concludes with an integrated writing or speaking task based on the authentic needs of the academic classroom. Units alternate between focusing on writing and speaking.

Before You Write/Speak introduces the language skill that students will need in the integrated task.

---

2. How does WVO compare to other fuels you have learned about? Explain your answers.

Example

In my opinion, WVO is better than other biofuels because . . .

3. What are some other solutions to our dependence on petroleum? What can we do as individuals and in our communities?

Checkpoint 2 myacademicconnectionslab

Before You Write

Writing a Problem-Solution Paragraph

A problem-solution paragraph describes a problem. Then it explains a solution or possible solutions to the problem. A problem-solution paragraph typically includes three parts:

- a topic sentence with a description of the problem
- a body with a description of (a) possible solution(s)
- a conclusion with an explanation of how the solution is helpful

Read a transcript from a talk given by Martyn Poliakoff, a chemist at the University of Nottingham. Then answer the questions on page 94.

4
Building Academic Writing Skills

In this section, you will practice writing problem-solution paragraphs. Then you will write a paragraph about a modern problem related to green chemistry. You will synthesize information and use vocabulary from the readings and the lecture. For online assignments, go to myacademicconnectionslab

Taking Green Chemistry to the Developing World

Recently I was asked to introduce the ideas of green chemistry to a group of high school students and teachers at Wachamo Comprehensive High School in Hossana, Ethiopia. The problem was that I wasn't sure of the best way to explain green chemistry simply. My solution was to use an example of a plastic bag that I got two days earlier at the town's market. They make bags like these from petroleum from other countries, because Ethiopia does not have much petroleum of its own. After people use these bags, they throw them away. On the road I counted 12 bags that people had thrown away in just 100 meters on my way to the school. By contrast, Ethiopia produces a lot of of sugarcane. If people there made the bags from sugarcane, then Ethiopia would not have to buy its bags—or oil to make bags—from other countries. More

(continued on next page)

Before you Speak

Presenting a Role Play

In academic classes you may be asked to create and perform a role play (short drama) to demonstrate your understanding of concepts you learn. Use these techniques to help make your performance more effective:

- Memorize the content of your role play—do not read it.
- Make note of nonverbal signals to use throughout your performance.
- Practice several times.
- Face your audience.
- Use a loud voice so that everyone can hear you clearly.
- Pay attention to stress and intonation in your voice.

4
Building Academic Speaking Skills

In this section, you will practice preparing role plays. You will also practice using stress, intonation, and pauses to express meaning. Then you will use ideas and vocabulary from this unit to write and present a role play demonstrating the importance of nonverbal communication. For online assignments, go to myacademicconnectionslab

1. Work with a partner. Complete the dialogue based on the COPS video scene you read about on pages 145–146. Practice the dialogue with your partner, using the techniques in the skill box.

Example

WOMAN: Oh, no! He was SHOT! Oh! . . .

POLICE OFFICER: Now calm down. I need you to . . .

WOMAN: Where are they taking him? I've got to . . .

2. Perform the role play for another pair of students. As you watch your classmates' performance, make a note of one thing they did well and one thing they could have done better.

Focused Speaking

1. Read the article about proxemics, a form of nonverbal communication that studies personal space.

PROXEMICS FOR BETTER COMMUNICATION

The distance people keep between themselves and others expresses their level of comfort together and the closeness of their relationship. As the diagram shows, intimate space—the zone very near the body—is usually for people with whom we have a very close relationship, such as romantic partners. On the other hand, space farther away from the body is used with people we do not know as well. This idea is generally universal, though the exact distances vary from culture to culture and person to person.

Focused Writing

1. Read the advice from marketing entrepreneur Bob Leduc on how businesses can find their niche markets. Underline the most important ideas. Then work with a partner. Discuss the most important ideas of the excerpt. What is its general purpose?

A Niche of Your Own: *Finding a Niche Market*
by Bob Leduc

1. First, list all the benefits that your product or service gives. For example, a product might save time, save money, or give pleasure.
2. List some of the characteristics of customers who would benefit from your product.
3. Decide if the group you've identified is profitable and if you can connect with it. If so, you should be able to answer YES to these questions:

   ■ Do your target customers have a strong need for your product or service?
   ■ Do they have money to pay for your product or service?
   ■ Is this group big enough to give you enough business?
   ■ Can you find ways to reach your niche through marketing and ads?
   ■ Can you clearly explain your product/service to these customers and persuade them of its benefits?

If you answer YES to all these questions, you've found a successful niche market!

Source: Adapted from Leduc, B. (1999). Target a niche market to increase your sales and profits. Retrieved May 27, 2009, from http://www.soha.org/Marketing-Articles/Target-a-Niche.htm.

Understanding How Audience Affects Purpose

When preparing to write or speak, think about your audience—the people you are writing or speaking to. Understanding your audience can influence your purpose and affect how you present information. To help identify your audience, think about these questions:

- Who will be your readers? (children, men, students, parents, etc.)
- What do you know about them? (gender, interests, feelings toward topic, education level, etc.)

Use what you know about your audience to identify your own purpose and to choose the best techniques for sharing information. Here are some examples:

- If your audience has opinions that are different from yours, you may try to persuade them.
- If your audience has little knowledge of your subject, you may need to inform them about it or explain it to them.
- If your audience has little interest in your subject, it may be helpful to entertain them as you give information.

Focused Writing/Speaking
explains the skill that will be used in the integrated task. Students use the additional reading or listening selection in this section to practice the skill and prepare for the integrated task activity.

Focused Speaking

Preparing for an Oral Presentation, Cont'd

You can use certain expressions to help your listeners follow your presentation.
To introduce your main idea or topic:
  Today I am going to talk about . . .
  My presentation today is on . . .
To introduce a point:
  First/Second, . . .
  Next, . . .
  Another cause/effect is . . .
  Finally, . . .
  My final point is . . .
To conclude your presentation:
  In conclusion, . . .
  To close, . . .
To ask if there are any questions from your listeners:
  Are there any questions?
  Do you have any questions?

1. ⟨∩⟩ Listen again to the presentation in Before You Speak on page 32. Check (✓) the expressions you hear.

_____ Today I am going to talk about . . .

_____ My presentation today is on . . .

_____ First, . . .

_____ Second, . . .

_____ Next, . . .

_____ Another cause is . . .

_____ Another effect is . . .

_____ Finally, . . .

_____ My final point, . . .

_____ In conclusion, . . .

_____ To close, . . .

_____ Are there any questions?

_____ Do you have any questions?

The **Integrated Writing/Speaking Task** challenges students to organize and synthesize information from the reading and listening selections in a meaningful way. Students follow clear steps that require them to use the vocabulary and academic skills they have learned in the unit. Completing the task is a productive achievement that gives students the tools and the confidence needed for academic success.

5. *Use your outline to write a paragraph. Use the paragraphs on pages 4 and 13 as examples. Then share your paragraphs in small groups.*

Integrated Writing Task

You have read a text about first impressions and listened to a lecture about elements of attraction. You will now listen to a conversation between two students meeting for the first time. You will use your knowledge of the unit content, topic vocabulary, and paragraph writing to write a paragraph in which you make a prediction about the relationship between the students.

1. ⌒ *Listen to the conversation between Akiko and Rosa. Who does each item in the chart apply to? Check (✓) the name(s). Then compare your answers with a partner's.*

Who . . .	Akiko	Rosa
1. is a new student?		
2. knows Hiro?		
3. wears nice clothes?		
4. is helping at the orientation?		
5. will show the cafeteria?		
6. will buy coffee?		
7. likes to shop?		

2. *Each sentence illustrates a main point from the unit. Label the sentences with the words and phrases from the box. Then compare your answers with a partner's.*

beauty	first impression	self-fulfilling prophecy
exchange	primacy effect	similarity

1. Rosa and Akiko both like to shop. _____

2. Hiro tells Rosa that Akiko is nice. Rosa expects Akiko to be nice. _____

3. When Rosa meets Akiko, she notices that she is nice, has short hair, and is well dressed. _____

4. Rosa thinks Akiko's bag looks very nice. _____

5. Rosa shows Akiko the cafeteria. Akiko buys Rosa coffee. _____

6. Rosa doesn't notice when Akiko does something wrong. _____

Integrated Speaking Task

You have read about the common elements of folktales, read and heard several folktales, and read and heard a model narrative summary. You will now use your knowledge of the unit content, topic vocabulary, and strategies for summarizing to give an oral narrative summary of a folktale you know.

Follow the steps to prepare for your presentation.

Step 1: Think of a folktale you know, or use the library or Internet to find one. Review the folktale and make sure you understand it well. (***Note:*** You can use the folktale you shared in Exercise 4 on page 65.)

Step 2: Complete the chart with information about your folktale.

Title and origin	
Time	
Place	
Characters	
Problem	
Main events of plot	
How problem is solved	

Step 3: Use your notes and review the skill box on page 74 and the guidelines and expressions on pages 75–76 to outline a narrative summary of your folktale. Use the summary of *The Tree with the Golden Apples* on page 75 as a model.

- In your opening sentence, introduce the common elements of folktales discussed in the lecture: the culture or tradition in which the story is based, the main characters, and the main problem in the plot.

MyAcademicConnectionsLab

MyAcademicConnectionsLab, an integral part of the *Academic Connections* series, is an easy-to-use online program that delivers personalized instruction and practice to students and rich resources to teachers.

- Students can access reading and listening selections, do practice activities, and prepare for tests anytime they go online.
- Teachers can take advantage of many resources including online assessments, a flexible gradebook, and tools for monitoring student progress.

The **MyAcademicConnectionsLab** WELCOME page organizes assignments and grades, and facilitates communication between students and teachers. It also allows the teacher to monitor student progress.

For Sections 1–3, MyAcademicConnectionsLab provides Vocabulary Check activities. These activities assess students' knowledge of the vocabulary needed for comprehension of the content and follow up with individualized instruction.

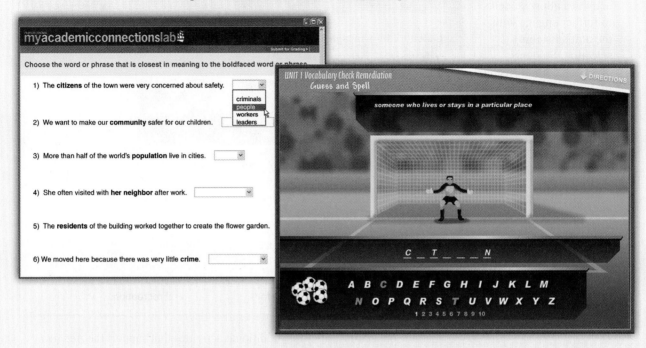

Reading and listening selections from the student book and additional practice activities are available to students online. Students benefit from virtually unlimited practice anywhere, anytime.

- Reading-based activities allow students to further engage with the unit's reading selection. Students practice comprehension, academic skills, grammar, and content vocabulary.

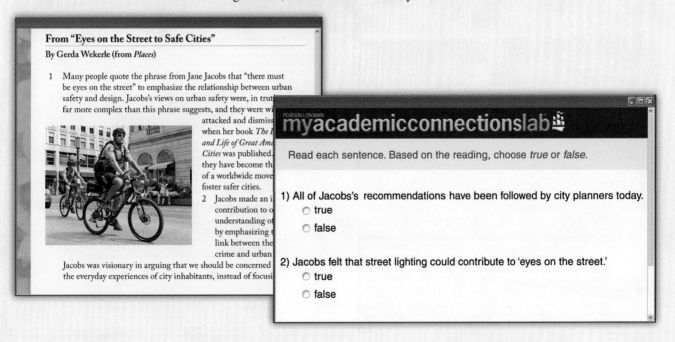

- Listening-based activities allow students to further engage with the unit's listening selection. Students practice comprehension, listening skills, and note-taking skills.

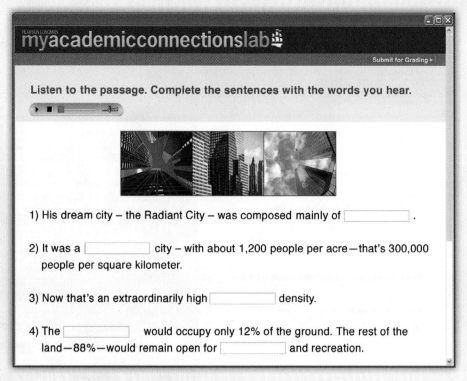

MyAcademicConnectionsLab offers additional activities that support the *Academic Connections* program.
- Fun, interactive games reinforce academic vocabulary and skills.
- Internet-based and discussion-board activities expand students' knowledge of the topic and help them practice new vocabulary.

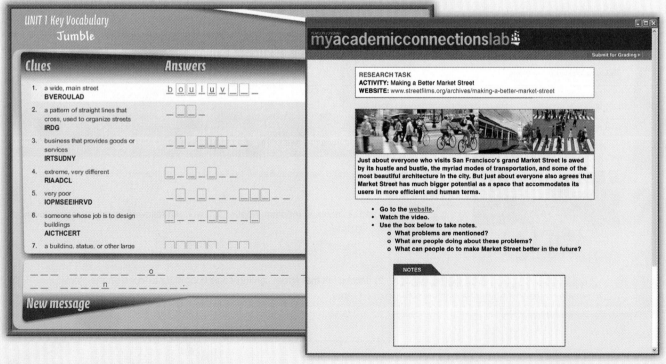

The MyAcademicConnectionsLab ASSESSMENT tools allow instructors to customize and deliver tests online.

- A placement test situates students in the appropriate level (also available in the paper format).
- Pre-course and post-course tests allow teachers to target instruction.
- Section tests monitor student progress.

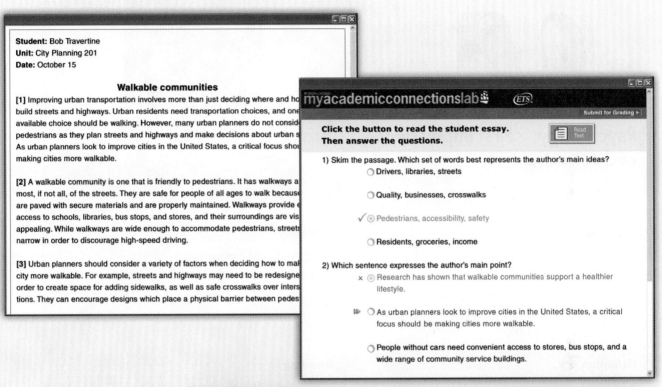

Teacher support materials in MyAcademic ConnectionsLab offer tips and suggestions for teaching the *Academic Connections* material and makes lesson planning easier.

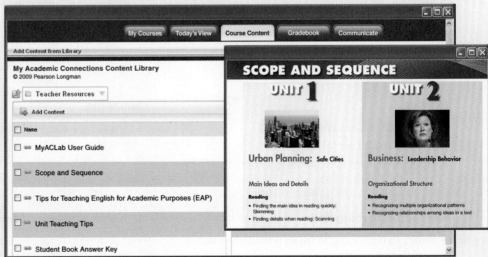

SCOPE AND SEQUENCE

UNIT 1

Psychology: First Impressions and Attraction

Main Ideas and Supporting Details

Reading

- Finding the main idea
- Skimming for main ideas
- Scanning for supporting details

Listening

- Listening for main ideas
- Using outlines
- Listening for details

Writing

- Recognizing parts of a paragraph
- Writing a topic sentence
- Using an outline to organize a paragraph

Integrated Writing Task

- Writing a paragraph to make a prediction about a relationship

UNIT 2

Ecology: The Web of Life

Organizational Structure

Listening

- Organizing information
- Listening for cause-and-effect expressions

Reading

- Cause-and-effect organization: block organization

Speaking

- Preparing for an oral presentation

Integrated Speaking Task

- Preparing an oral presentation about the causes and effects of the degradation of an ecosystem service

UNIT 3

Health: Stress and Health

Coherence and Cohesion

Reading
- Recognizing coherence in texts
- Using connectors for cohesion
- Using transition words for cohesion

Listening
- Listening for organization: Speech markers
- Listening for examples

Writing
- Planning a coherent paragraph
- Using cohesive expressions

Integrated Writing Task
- Writing a cohesive and coherent paragraph about technostress

UNIT 4

Literature: Folktales

Summarizing

Listening
- Recognizing summary statements
- Distinguishing major from minor points

Reading
- Using time-order words
- Paraphrasing

Speaking
- Preparing narrative summaries
- Giving a narrative summary

Integrated Speaking Task
- Preparing and presenting an oral summary of a folktale

UNIT 5

Chemistry: Green Chemistry

Synthesizing Information

Reading

- Recognizing relationships between different pieces of information
- Recognizing the relationship between abstract concepts and concrete information

Listening

- Recognizing the relationship between two spoken sources

Writing

- Writing a problem-solution paragraph
- Introducing problems and solutions

Integrated Writing Task

- Writing a problem-solution paragraph

UNIT 6

Art History: The Art of Marc Chagall

Fact and Opinion

Reading

- Identifying facts
- Identifying opinions

Listening

- Recognizing a speaker's degree of certainty
- Identifying support for opinions

Speaking

- Giving and supporting an opinion
- Showing agreement and disagreement

Integrated Speaking Task

- Participating in a group discussion about a painting by Marc Chagall

UNIT 7

Marketing: Niche Marketing

Purpose

Reading

- Recognizing general purpose
- Recognizing persuasive language

Listening

- Recognizing specific purpose
- Understanding meaning through intonation and stress

Writing

- Writing a persuasive paragraph
- Understanding how audience affects purpose

Integrated Writing Task

- Writing a letter persuading someone to invest in a business

UNIT 8

Communication: Nonverbal Communication

Inference

Listening

- Making inferences about a speaker's attitude

Reading

- Inferring word meaning from context

Speaking

- Presenting a role play
- Using stress, intonation, and pauses to express meaning

Integrated Speaking Task

- Preparing and participating in a role play demonstrating nonverbal communication

ACKNOWLEDGMENTS

The authors would like to acknowledge with gratitude the people who worked closely on this project with us: Debbie Sistino, John Beaumont, and Mykan White. The vision and determination of Debbie, John, Sherry Preiss and others shaped the series in general and this book in particular. We especially appreciate the fresh perspective, intelligent insight, and creative activity ideas and feedback of Mykan White. We would also like to thank Gosia Jaros-White, development editor, for her attention to detail and coherence, and Sherry Preiss for her enthusiasm and support.

We appreciate the many friends, colleagues and reviewers who discussed content and activities with us: Lisa Belluzzi, UCSB; Steve Palladino, Ventura College; Craig Martinsen, to name a few; and our ESL students at Santa Barbara City College, who inform our teaching and writing every day.

We wish to express deep gratitude for our families, Wayne, Christopher, Brian, Eric, our moms and mothers-and-fathers-in-law for supporting us in more ways than we can express. We are also grateful to welcome the long-awaited, new family member of Marit and Eric, who has been growing right alongside this project.

Finally, the authors extend heartfelt thanks and love to each other for engaging in a challenging project that required a lot of patience, countless late nights, and inspiring collaboration.

Betsy Cassriel
Marit ter-Mate Martinsen

The publisher would like to thank the following people.

Matthew Chametzky, R&D Capability Manager at ETS, who coordinated all assessment work for this project, bringing order when chaos seemed imminent.

Terry Cryan, Assessment Specialist at ETS who helped us all better understand (and appreciate) the many differences between testing and teaching.

Kate Kazin, Director of Client Management at ETS, whose clear vision kept the project true to its objective of evidence-based design.

REVIEWERS

For the comments and insights they graciously offered to help shape the direction of *Academic Connections*, the publisher would like to thank the following reviewers and institutions.

Donette Artenie, Georgetown University; **Jennifer Castello**, Cañada College; **Carol A. Chapelle**, Iowa State University; **JoAnn (Jodi) Crandall**, University of Maryland; **Wendy Crockett**, J. W. North High School; **Lois Darlington**, Columbia University; **Christopher Davis**, John Jay College; **Robert Dickey**, Gyeongju University, Gyeongju, Korea; **Deborah B. Gordon**, Santa Barbara City College; **Mike Hammond**, University of California, San Diego; **Ian Hosack**, Ritsumeikan University, Kyoto; **Sylvie Huneault-Schultze**, Fresno City College; **Barbara Inerfeld**, Rutgers University; **Joan Jamieson**, Northern Arizona University; **Scott Jenison**, Antelope Valley College; **Mandy Kama**, Georgetown University; **Dr. Jose Lai**, The Chinese University of Hong Kong; **Rama Mathew**, Delhi University, Delhi, India; **Mitchell Mirkin**, Baltimore City Community College; **Carla Billings Nyssen**, California State University, Long Beach; **Yannick O'Neill**, Gyeongnam Education Board, Changwon, South Korea; **Gretchen Owens**, San Francisco State University; **Angela Parrino**, Hunter College; **Sarah C. Saxer**, Howard Community College; **Diane Schmitt**, Nottingham Trent University, Nottingham U.K.; **Gail Schmitt**, Montgomery College; **Fred Servito**, University of Washington; **Janet Shanks Van Suntum**, Fordham University, Pace University; **Karen Shimoda**, Freelance ESL Development Editor; **Dean E. Stafford**, Sanho Elementary School, Mason, South Korea; **Fredricka L. Stoller**, Northern Arizona University; **Richmond Stroupe**, Soka University, Tokyo; **Jessica Williams**, University of Illinois; **Kirsten Windahl**, Cuyahoga Community College

UNIT 1

Psychology
First Impressions and Attraction

Unit Description

Content: This course is designed to familiarize the student with concepts in social psychology.

Skills: Main Ideas and Supporting Details

- Finding the main idea
- Skimming for main ideas
- Scanning for supporting details
- Listening for main ideas
- Using outlines
- Listening for details
- Recognizing parts of a paragraph
- Writing a topic sentence
- Using an outline to organize a paragraph

Unit Requirements

Reading: "The Power of First Impressions" (an excerpt from a scientific journal)

Lecture: "Elements of Attraction"

Listening: "A First Meeting" (a campus conversation)

Integrated Writing Task: Writing a paragraph to make a prediction about a relationship

Assignments: www.MyAcademicConnectionsLab.com

1

1

Preview

For online assignments, go to

PEARSON LONGMAN
myacademicconnectionslab

Key Words

attraction *n* the feeling of liking someone very much; **attractive** *adj*

impression *n* an opinion or feeling about someone

interact *v* to talk to other people or to work together with them

notice *v* to see, hear, or smell something

opinion *n* an idea or belief about something

Previewing Academic Content

Things and people are not always what they seem. But studies show that first impressions—what people think of each other when they first meet—can greatly help or hurt a relationship. Feelings of attraction can also make relationships successful or unsuccessful. But how do people form first impressions, and why are first impressions important? What causes attraction between two people? In this unit, you will learn the answers to these questions.

1. *How do you form a first impression about a person? Check (✓) three things you notice.*

_____ way of talking _____ clothes and accessories _____ face

_____ hair _____ posture (how a person sits or stands) _____ body shape

Dr. Marianne LaFrance,[1] a psychology professor at Yale University, conducted a study on first impressions and hairstyles. She asked participants to describe people in 300 photos. La France gave each person only two seconds to form an impression.

2. *Look at each photo. Then complete the chart. How well does each adjective describe the person? For each person, number each adjective from 1 to 5. Number 1 means the adjective describes the person very well. Number 5 means the adjective does not describe the person at all. Work quickly!*

	Attractive	Confident	Friendly	Intelligent	Selfish

---

[1] Adapted from "First Impressions and Hair Impressions: An Investigation of Impact of Hair Style on First Impressions." Marianne LaFrance. February 2001.

3. *Compare your answers in Exercise 2 with a partner's. Then discuss the questions.*

1. What did you first notice about the people in the photos (for example, eyes, hair, smile)?

2. What was your first impression of each person?

3. Which person do you find most attractive? Why?

4. Which person would you most like to meet? Why?

This unit will help you recognize main ideas and details in readings and lectures. It will also help you to write clearly with main ideas and details.

Previewing the Academic Skills Focus

1. *Read a paragraph from a psychology textbook. Underline the sentence that you think is the author's most important idea or point.*

Forming First Impressions

People are very good at forming first impressions from little information. Just seeing someone's face or hearing someone speak can affect how we think about him or her. Clothing and hairstyle can also affect our feelings. We even form opinions about a person's body and posture. We form these early ideas about others very quickly, often without meaning to or knowing what we are doing.

2. *Compare the sentence you have underlined with a partner's.*

- Did you both underline the same sentence?
- What is the most important idea in this paragraph?

Main Ideas and Supporting Details

In this unit, you will learn to find and use main ideas and supporting details. A main idea is the most important idea about the topic. Supporting details are small pieces of information that help explain the main idea. Learning to find main ideas and supporting details will help you understand college reading assignments and class lectures.

3. *Read the paragraph again. Discuss how the other sentences help to explain and support the main idea. What kind of information does each sentence give?*

2

Building Academic Reading Skills

In this section, you will learn how to read for main ideas and details. You will also practice skimming and scanning. For online assignments, go to

PEARSON LONGMAN
myacademicconnectionslab

Before You Read

1. *Use the key words to complete the statements.*

1. The first time two people meet can have a very strong _____ on a relationship.

2. People usually act or _____ in the way other people _____ them to act.

3. When you meet someone new, it is easy to make a _____ about your future relationship.

4. A first impression can _____ a relationship more than later impressions.

Compare your answers with a partner's. Then discuss the statements. Do you agree or disagree?

Key Words

behave *v* to do or say things in a particular way

expect *v* to believe strongly that something will happen; **expectation** *n*

impact *n* the effect that an event or situation has on someone or something

influence *v* to have an effect on the way someone or something behaves, thinks, or develops

prediction *n* a guess about what is going to happen; **predict** *v*

Finding the Main Idea

As you have learned, the main idea is the most important idea of a text. It gives general information about a topic. Other sentences in the text provide supporting details.

You can usually find the main idea of a paragraph in the title (or paragraph heading) or in the first or last sentence of the paragraph.

2. *Read the paragraph about schemata from a psychology textbook.*

The Importance of Schemata

When people meet someone for the first time, they form a fast impression about that person by putting her or him into a familiar category or group. They use schemata to help form these impressions. Schemata are ideas and expectations about a group based on past experiences (Aronson, Wilson, & Ackert, 2005). For instance, if someone sees a woman wearing a white coat and a stethoscope[1] around her neck, he will probably think she is a doctor. He will think this woman is like other doctors he knows. For example, he may think she is well educated and knows about disease and medicine. Organizing people into familiar groups like this is a common way that people form first impressions very quickly.

---

[1] **stethoscope** *n* an instrument that a doctor uses to listen to your heart or breathing

Aronson, E., Wilson, T.D., & Eckert, R.M. (2005). *Social psychology* (5th ed). Upper Saddle River, New Jersey: Pearson Prentice Hall.

3. *Work with a partner. Write* **MI** *next to the statement that gives the main idea of the paragraph. Then underline the sentence in the paragraph that best expresses this main idea.*

_____ A woman in a white coat is probably a doctor.

_____ Schemata are helpful in forming fast first impressions.

_____ Ideas and expectations based on past experiences are called schemata.

4. *How did you find the main idea? Check (✓) your answer(s).*

_____ It is general and important to the paragraph.

_____ The other sentences give supporting details.

_____ It is in the paragraph heading/title.

_____ It is in the first sentence.

_____ It is in the last sentence.

Compare your answers in small groups. Why are the other two statements in Exercise 3 not the main idea?

Global Reading

Skimming for Main Ideas

Skimming is reading quickly to find main ideas in a short time. Skimming before you read will prepare you to read and understand the passage better. To skim for main ideas, look at:
- the title
- repeated ideas and words
- the first and last sentences (in paragraphs)
- the first and last paragraphs (in longer texts)

When skimming, do <u>not</u>:
- read every word or sentence
- look up words you don't know

1. *The reading in this section is an article from a scientific journal. Skim the text on page 6. Circle the number of the paragraph that includes the main idea of the entire text. Underline the sentence that states the main idea. Then read the entire article.*

The Power of First Impressions

1   When people meet for the first time, they make first impressions of one another in a few seconds. To do this, they notice clothes, body shape, the way a person talks, and expressions he or she makes. Research shows that first impressions are very important because they have a strong impact on forming relationships.

2   Studies show that the *primacy effect* is an important part of first impressions. The primacy effect is the idea that the first impression is very difficult to change. After the first meeting, two people may interact again and learn more about each other, but the early impressions they formed will influence their feelings about each other in the future. For example, if a person has a good first impression of someone, he or she probably will not notice bad things about the person later. However, if that person has a bad first impression, he or she will probably notice mostly bad things in the future.

3   Another interesting part of first impressions is that people act how others expect them to act. This is called a *self-fulfilling prophecy*. Research by Snyder and Swann supports this idea (1978). In that study, partners played a game together. The partners did not know one another, so the researchers told each player about his partner. Sometimes they said positive, or good, things about a partner. Sometimes they said negative, or bad, things. The result of the study showed that players acted friendly when they expected their partners to be friendly, but they acted unfriendly when they expected their partners to be unfriendly. (See Figure 1.1) The players' expectations influenced how they acted toward one another.

SELF-FULFILLING PROPHECY	
A expects B to be friendly	A expects B to be unfriendly
A is friendly to B	A is unfriendly to B
B is friendly to A	B is unfriendly to A

Figure 1.1

4   A related study by Michael Sunnafrank (2004) showed that when people first meet, they quickly make predictions about what kind of relationship they will have. Sunnafrank found that these predictions had a strong impact on future relationships. In his study of 164 first-year college students, Sunnafrank found that when students predicted they could be friends, they sat closer together in class and interacted more. As a result, they actually became friends. In other words, they made their predictions come true.

5   Clearly, first impressions are very important in forming relationships, because they influence the expectations people have of one another and how they behave toward one another.

Snyder, M., & Swann, W.B. (1978). Behavioral confirmation in social interaction: From social perception to social reality. *Journal of Experimental Social Psychology, 14*, 148–162.

Sunnafrank, M., & Ramirez, A. (2004). At first sight: Persistent relational effects of get-acquainted conversations. *Journal of Social and Personal Relationships, 21*(3), 361–379.

2. Skim each paragraph again. Match each paragraph with its main idea. (Note: Two paragraphs have the same main idea.)

_____ Paragraph 1

_____ Paragraph 2

_____ Paragraph 3

_____ Paragraph 4

_____ Paragraph 5

a. People's expectations can influence how a person acts.

b. First impressions are very important in forming relationships.

c. A first impression is not easy to change.

d. People act on their predictions to make the relationship they expect.

3. Circle the correct answer.

1. Why are first impressions important?
   a. They help people notice specific things about others.
   b. They influence relationships.

2. Which statement describes the primacy effect?
   a. People act how other people expect them to act.
   b. First impressions do not change very much.

3. Which statement describes self-fulfilling prophecy?
   a. People act how other people expect them to act.
   b. First impressions do not change very much.

4. According to Sunnafrank's study, what happens after people make predictions about a relationship?
   a. People's predictions do not affect their actions.
   b. People act to make the predictions come true.

5. Which idea does Sunnafrank's study support?
   a. self-fulfilling prophecy
   b. primacy effect

Focused Reading

Scanning for Supporting Details

Scanning is very fast reading for details, such as examples, reasons, and definitions. When you scan, look for the answer to a specific question. Move your eyes quickly, and look only for specific information that will answer the question.

To answer questions about	Look for
who and where	capital letters and names
when	numbers, dates, and time periods
how much, how many, and how long	numbers and measurements (such as meters, inches, etc.)
what, how, and why	key word(s) or word(s) from the question

1. *Circle the question words in the Questions column of the chart. Then scan the reading on page 6 to answer the questions.*

Questions	Answers
1. How long does it take to make a first impression?	*a few seconds*
2. What are four things people notice when they first meet someone?	
3. When did Snyder and Swan complete their study?	
4. Who studied people's predictions about relationships?	
5. How many first-year college students were in Sunnafrank's study?	

2. *Discuss the questions in small groups.*

1. Describe a recent first impression you had of someone. What do you predict about your relationship with this person?

2. Have you ever experienced the primacy effect? Have you experienced self-fulfilling prophecy? If so, describe what happened.

3. Many studies show that students do better in school when teachers expect them to be good students. Why do you think it is important for teachers, parents, and administrators to understand the idea of self-fulfilling prophecy?

Checkpoint 1   ^{PEARSON LONGMAN} myacademicconnectionslab⚓

In this section, you will
practice listening for
and taking notes on the
main ideas and details
of a lecture.
For online assignments,
go to

**PEARSON LONGMAN
myacademicconnectionslab**

Key Words

element *n* one part of
a whole

physical *adj* relating to
the body, not the mind
or soul

quality *n* a part of
someone's personality

romantic *adj* showing
strong feelings of love

session *n* a meeting
for a particular purpose

similar *adj* almost the
same, but not exactly
the same; **similarity** *n*

Before You Listen

Peter M. Todd (2007), a psychologist from Indiana
University, studied speed dating to learn more about
elements of attraction. At speed-dating sessions, people
try to find a romantic partner—someone to have a
loving relationship with. Two people meet and talk for a
very short time. After three to 10 minutes, they move to
meet another person and so on. After that, they decide
which men or women they want to see again. In his
study, Todd wanted to find out two things:

- what qualities people said they wanted in a
  romantic partner
- what qualities really attracted people to each other during the
  speed-dating session

Todd studied how important certain qualities were to participants:

- similarity to themselves
- physical beauty
- having a good job
- the belief that family is important

Todd, P.M. et al. (2007). Different cognitive processes underlie human mate choices and mate
preferences. *PNAS, 104*(38), 15011–15016.

1. *What qualities are most important to you in a romantic partner? Number the
qualities in order of importance from 1 to 4. Number 1 is the most important,
and number 4 is the least important.*

_____ 1. a person who is similar to me

_____ 2. a person with physical beauty

_____ 3. a person with a good job

_____ 4. a person who thinks family is very important

2. *Work as a class to complete the chart. Write the number of men and women
in your class who wrote **1** for each item in Exercise 1. Then add up the total.
Do most people in your class agree on what is most important in a romantic
partner? Do men and women agree?*

Quality	Men	Women	Total
similar to me			
physical beauty			
good job			
family is very important			

3. *Discuss the questions in small groups.*

1. Which quality is most important to you in a romantic partner? Why?

2. Look at the chart of your classmates' answers in Exercise 2. Did anything surprise you? Why or why not?

3. In Todd's study, which qualities do you think the men said they wanted in a romantic partner? Which qualities do you think really attracted them to people during the speed-dating session?

4. In Todd's study, which qualities do you think the women said they wanted in a romantic partner? Which qualities do you think really attracted them to people during the speed-dating session?

5. Look at your answers to Exercise 1 on page 9. Would you number the qualities differently when choosing a friend instead of a romantic partner? Explain.

Global Listening

Listening for Main Ideas

The first step to understanding a lecture is to listen for main ideas. The main idea of an entire lecture often comes at the beginning (introduction) and/or end (conclusion) of a lecture. You will hear additional important ideas throughout the lecture.

To find main ideas in a lecture, listen for certain expressions:

Today's lecture is about . . .

I will talk about . . .

The most important idea here is . . .

Another important point is . . .

Note: Speakers often stress important ideas by speaking more slowly or more loudly.

1. 🎧 *Listen to the introduction of the lecture. What is the main idea of the lecture? Check (✓) your prediction.*

_____ 1. Interpersonal attraction is when a person wants a relationship with someone.

_____ 2. Three elements of interpersonal attraction are important in all relationships.

_____ 3. Relationships include those with friends, family, and romantic partners.

2. *Check (✓) the ways the professor shows the main idea.*

_____ 1. He gives the main idea at the beginning of the introduction.

_____ 2. He uses a certain expression to introduce the main idea.

_____ 3. He slows down his speech.

_____ 4. He speaks more loudly.

Using an **outline** is a good way to take notes on a reading assignment or a lecture. An outline is a list of main ideas. Each main idea is followed by a list of supporting details. Students often make their own outlines for note-taking, and some professors give students lecture outlines.

When using an outline, you don't have to write complete sentences. You can save time by using words, phrases (groups of words), and symbols (for example, %, =).

3. ⌒ *Listen to the whole lecture. Write the main ideas in the outline. Use words, phrases, and symbols where possible. You will take notes on the details—shown with bullets (•)—later.*

PSYCHOLOGY 101   *Professor John Watkins*
Elements of Attraction

(Introduction) *3 Important elements of attraction*

- *physical attractiveness*

- _____

- _____

(Main idea) _____

- *Peter Todd study:*

- *People believe that*

- *Teachers*

- _____

(Main idea) _____

- *People usually choose*

- _____ *more confident* ___

- *Peter Todd study:*

(Main idea) _____

- *Definition=*

- *2 people feel good about exchange=*

- _____

(Conclusion) _____

---

4. *Discuss your outline with the class and make any necessary changes.*

Focused Listening

As in a written text, the details in a lecture give more specific information about the main idea. Listening for details will help you understand the professor's main points. You can find different types of details by listening for these expressions:

Type of Detail	Expression
example	*for example, for instance, specifically*
reason	*because, since*
definition	*this is, this means*

1. 🎧 *Listen to the lecture again. Notice the expressions that introduce details. Complete the outline on page 11 by writing details. Then compare your outline with a partner's.*

2. *Discuss the details you wrote in the outline with a partner. Decide if each is an example, reason, or defintion. Then report back to the class.*

3. *Work with the same partner. Read the statements. Decide if they are true or false. Write **T** (true) or **F** (false). Use your outline on page 11 for help. If necessary, listen to the lecture again.*

_____ 1. Interpersonal attraction means wanting a relationship with another person.

_____ 2. The professor thinks that most people believe beauty is an important part of attraction.

_____ 3. People think that attractive people are more intelligent.

_____ 4. Mothers behave the same toward attractive and unattractive babies.

_____ 5. There are very few studies on similarity.

_____ 6. People usually like to be with other people who are different.

_____ 7. Exchange is when one person takes something from someone else.

4. *Complete the chart. Connect ideas from the reading and lecture to a relationship you have had.*

Ideas from Reading and Lecture	My Relationship with _____
First impression: primacy effect, self-fulfilling prophecy, predicting	
Attraction: beauty, similarity, exchange	

5. *Work in small groups. Prepare and give a one- to two-minute presentation about your relationship. Use your notes and any of the phrases listed.*

- My first impression of [person's name] was that he/she was . . .
- When we first met, I predicted that we were going to . . .
- [Person's name] and I have a good/weak relationship because . . .

Example

My first impression of my roommate Ken was that he was lazy. When I first met him, it was noon, and he was sleeping. Also, his room was very messy. I predicted right away that we were not going to be great roomates, because I am a hard worker who likes to keep things clean. Ken is a friendly and helpful person, but I think I'll find a new roommate soon.

Checkpoint 2 myacademicconnectionslab

4
Building Academic Writing Skills

In this section, you will practice recognizing parts of a paragraph and writing topic sentences. Then you will write a paragraph making a prediction about the relationship between two students who are meeting for the first time. You will use ideas and vocabulary from this unit.
For online assignments, go to

myacademicconnectionslab

Before You Write

Recognizing Parts of a Paragraph

A paragraph is a group of sentences about the same main idea. An academic paragraph usually has three parts:
1. A **topic sentence** that introduces the main idea.
2. A **body** with supporting details that help explain the main idea.
3. A **concluding sentence** that reviews the main idea or makes a final comment.

1. *Read the textbook paragraph. Underline the topic sentence once, check (✓) the supporting details, and underline the concluding sentence twice.*

Stereotypes

Stereotypes can influence first impressions in many ways, and they can also cause problems. A stereotype is a strong idea about what a person is like based on one thing, such as the person's age, sex, race, or job. People usually learn stereotypes at a young age, with ideas they get from family members, friends, television, and movies. When people use stereotypes to form first impressions, they expect the person to behave a certain way because of the stereotype. For example, they may expect a woman to be a good cook or a man to be strong. Because of their stereotypes, people may believe these things without paying attention to differences between people. As a result, they may be incorrect in their impressions. This can hurt a relationship.

Source: Morris, C.G., & Maitson, A.A. (2008). *Understanding psychology* (8th ed.) Upper Saddle River, NJ: Pearson Prentice Hall.

---

2. Complete the outline of the paragraph on page 13. Then work in small groups to compare outlines.

⊙ (Topic Sentence) _____

    (Body/Details)

      • _____

      • _____

      • _____

      • _____

⊙ (Concluding Sentence) _____

Focused Writing

Writing a Topic Sentence

The **topic sentence** introduces the main idea. When you write a topic sentence, always include these two parts:
- A **topic**—who or what the paragraph is about
- A **controlling idea**—what you want to say about the topic

The controlling idea often gives a feeling or opinion about the topic. Examples of opinion and feeling words are *important, special, good, bad,* and *interesting*.

Example

                       Opinion Word
                           ↓

(Stereotypes) can cause important problems when forming relationships.
      ↑   ↓
   Topic   **Controlling Idea**

1. Work with a partner. For each sentence, circle the topic and underline the controlling idea. Check (✓) the opinion/feeling words.

1. First impressions are important in forming relationships.

2. Physical attractiveness is more important to men than to women.

3. Expecting your children to behave badly in a situation can be a self-fulfilling prophecy.

4. My friend and I have a good exchange.

5. Stereotypes can have a great influence on first impressions.

2. *Work in small groups. Add controlling ideas to each topic to make one topic sentence.*

Examples

Beauty <u>is more important to men than to women.</u>

In my opinion, <u>the most important thing in a relationship is similarity.</u>

1. First impressions

   • _____

2. Beauty

   • _____

3. Self-fulfilling prophecy

   • _____

4. Similarity

   • _____

Using an Outline to Organize a Paragraph

Using an outline is an excellent way to organize your ideas before writing a paragraph. List the main ideas in the topic sentence. Indent and use bullets for the details. Then use the outline to write your paragraph.

3. *Work with a partner from your group. Write a paragraph outline in your notebook. Use the outline on page 14 as an example. Follow the steps.*
   • Choose a topic sentence from Exercise 2. Write it in the outline.
   • Write three supporting details about your main idea.
   • Write a concluding sentence that reviews your main idea.

4. *Work with two partners from another group. Compare outlines. Use the checklist to help you. Can you suggest any changes?*

Outline Checklist

_____ Does the topic sentence introduce the main idea?

_____ Does the topic sentence have a topic?

_____ Does the topic sentence have a controlling idea?

_____ Do the supporting details help explain the main idea?

_____ Does the concluding sentence review the main idea or make a final comment?

5. *Use your outline to write a paragraph. Use the paragraphs on pages 4 and 13 as examples. Then share your paragraphs in small groups.*

Integrated Writing Task

You have read a text about first impressions and listened to a lecture about elements of attraction. You will now listen to a conversation between two students meeting for the first time. You will use your knowledge of the unit content, topic vocabulary, and paragraph writing to write a paragraph in which you make a prediction about the relationship between the students.

1. 🎧 *Listen to the conversation between Akiko and Rosa. Who does each item in the chart apply to? Check (✓) the name(s). Then compare your answers with a partner's.*

Who . . .	Akiko	Rosa
1. is a new student?		
2. knows Hiro?		
3. wears nice clothes?		
4. is helping at the orientation?		
5. will show the cafeteria?		
6. will buy coffee?		
7. likes to shop?		

2. *Each sentence illustrates a main point from the unit. Label the sentences with the words and phrases from the box. Then compare your answers with a partner's.*

beauty	first impression	self-fulfilling prophecy
exchange	primacy effect	similarity

1. Rosa and Akiko both like to shop. _____

2. Hiro tells Rosa that Akiko is nice. Rosa expects Akiko to be nice.

   _____

3. When Rosa meets Akiko, she notices that she is nice, has short hair, and is well dressed. _____

4. Rosa thinks Akiko's bag looks very nice. _____

5. Rosa shows Akiko the cafeteria. Akiko buys Rosa coffee.

   _____

6. Rosa doesn't notice when Akiko does something wrong.

   _____

3. *Follow the steps to write your paragraph.*

Step 1: Based on the conversation you heard and your answers in Exercise 2, write a prediction about Rosa and Akiko's relationship. Use this phrase to begin the sentence:

I predict / My prediction is that they will _____.

Step 2: Write an outline for a paragraph explaining your prediction.
- Include a topic sentence, supporting details, and a concluding sentence. Use information from Rosa and Akiko's conversation and the reading and lecture in the unit.
- Review the skill box on page 13 to make sure the parts of your paragraph are complete.
- Review the skill box on page 14 to make sure your topic sentence is strong.

Step 3: Use your outline to write a paragraph.

Step 4: Exchange paragraphs with a partner. In the paragraph:
- Underline the topic sentence once.
- Circle the controlling idea.
- Check (✓) the supporting details.
- Underline the concluding sentence twice.

Then use the checklist to comment on your partner's paragraph.

Paragraph Checklist	Yes	No
Does the paragraph have a topic sentence that introduces the main idea?		
Does the topic sentence have a topic?		
Does the topic sentence have a controlling idea?		
Do the supporting details explain the main idea?		
Does the paragraph use the information from the conversation, reading, and lecture?		
Does the concluding sentence review the main idea and make a final comment?		

Step 5: Rewrite your paragraph based on your partner's comments. Then share your paragraphs in small groups. How are your predictions similar? How are they different?

UNIT 2

Ecology

The Web of Life

Unit Description

Content: This course is designed to familiarize the student with concepts in ecology and ecosystems.

Skills: Organizational Structure

- Organizing information
- Listening for cause-and-effect expressions
- Cause-and-effect organization: block organization
- Preparing for an oral presentation

Unit Requirements

Lecture: "Web of Life"

Reading: "Nature's Services—What Are They Worth?" (an excerpt from a scientific journal)

Listening: "The Disappearance of Honeybees" (a student presentation)

Integrated Speaking Task: Preparing an oral presentation about the causes and effects of the degradation of an ecosystem service

Assignments: www.MyAcademicConnectionsLab.com

1

Preview

For online assignments, go to

myacademicconnectionslab

Key Words

connected *adj* related or joined

depend on *v* to need something

ecosystem *n* all the animals and plants in a particular area, and the way in which they are related to each other and to their environment

environment *n* the world of land, sea, and air that a plant or animal lives in

provide *v* to give something to someone or make it available to them because they need it or want it

value *n* the importance or usefulness of something; *v* to think that something is useful or important

Previewing the Academic Content

Earth is home to millions of kinds of people, plants, and animals. They live together and interact to form different ecosystems. Like a spider's web, everything in our environment is connected. If one part of the web breaks, it influences the whole web. In this unit, you will study the web of life on Earth and our place in it. You will learn how a healthy ecosystem works and what happens when part of an ecosystem changes. You will also discover what products and services ecosystems provide to people. Finally, you will find out the value of these services and what it costs us to keep them safe.

Look at the flier. Then discuss the questions in small groups.

1. What are the two examples of ecosystem services described in the flier?

2. What connection between people and ecosystems does the flier describe?

3. What other useful services or products do ecosystems provide?

ECOSYSTEM SERVICES

People around the world depend on ecosystems for many products and services. Some say that these products and services are worth $33 trillion.

Water Purification[1]

- Lakes, rivers, and forests are all important for making water pure.

- Unhealthy things come out of water as it travels through these ecosystems.

- This natural water purification provides clean water for people and other living things to use and enjoy.

Pollination[2]

- Most plants with flowers need pollination to produce fruit and seeds.

- More than 100,000 different kinds of insects, birds, and animals pollinate plants.

- Many important food crops depend on pollination.

---

[1] *Purification* takes away the dirty or unhealthy parts from something, thus making it *pure*, or clean.

[2] *Pollination* is when a flower or plant gets pollen so that it can produce seeds.

In Unit 1, you learned how to recognize and use main ideas and details. This unit will help you recognize how writers and speakers organize such information. You will also learn how to understand and use cause-and-effect organization.

Previewing the Academic Skills Focus

Organizational Structure

As you learned in Unit 1, academic texts and lectures often have three main parts: an introduction, a body, and a conclusion. The way these ideas are organized is the **organizational structure**. Organizational structure is related to a writer or speaker's purpose. For example, someone may use a compare/contrast structure to tell how things are the same or different. Recognizing organizational structures will make reading and listening faster and easier.

In this unit, you will learn about the organizational structure of **cause and effect**. This structure is used to explain the relationship between a cause (the reason something happens) and the effect (the result of the cause).

1. *Study the cause and effect sentences. Underline the two parts in each sentence. Label the cause **C** and the effect **E**.*

Examples

        C   *E*

A change in one part of the web of life can lead to problems in other parts.

               E   *C*

Some ecosystems have changed due to human actions.

1. Pollination causes plants to make new seeds and fruit.

2. We need trees because they help clean the air.

3. Purification removes dirty parts from water so it is clean and healthy.

2. *Read the paragraphs. Then work with a partner to complete the tasks.*

> 1 Pollination is experiencing a serious problem because of changes in the ecosystems where many pollinators live. Birds, insects, and small animals that pollinate plants live in forests and other areas that humans are cutting down or hurting in other ways. As a result, the animals die or leave and cannot pollinate plants.
>
> 2 Losing pollinators will have serious effects for humans. One consequence is that we could have less food, because 70 percent of the world's food needs pollination to grow. Another effect is that businesses around the world could be hurt. Pollination around the world is worth many billions of dollars a year.

1. Underline the topic sentence of Paragraph 1. Put a check (✔) next to each supporting detail.

2. Circle the word that best completes the sentence:

    Paragraph 1 explains the *causes / effects* of losing pollination.

(continued on next page)

Key Words

cause *n* a person or thing that makes something happen; *v* to make something happen

consequence *n* something that happens as a result of something else

effect *n* a result

3. Underline the topic sentence of Paragraph 2. Put a check next to each supporting detail.

4. Circle the word that best completes the sentence:

   Paragraph 2 explains the ***causes / effects*** of losing pollination.

3. *Discuss your answers to items 2 and 4 in Exercise 2 with a partner.*

1. What information in the topic sentences you underlined helped you complete the statements?

2. Did the supporting details in the paragraphs help you complete these items? If so, how?

3. Did any special words in the paragraphs help you complete these items? If so, what were they?

Before You Listen

2

Building Academic Listening Skills

In this section, you will learn how to organize ideas, take notes while listening, and listen for causes and effects.
For online assignments, go to

PEARSON LONGMAN
myacademicconnectionslab

1. *Look at the diagram to identify the different parts of the ecosystem, and read the statements on the next page that describe the diagram. Label the statements in the correct order. Then compare your answers with a partner's.*

The Brazil nut tree grows in the Amazon rainforest. People eat Brazil nuts, and the international Brazil nut business is worth $50 million a year. To make new trees and new fruit, each tree needs the help of bees to pollinate.

_____ As a result of this pollination, there is new fruit.

_____ The agouti[1] opens the fruit to eat the nuts inside.

__1__ When bees visit the flowers of the tree to eat, pollen gets on their bodies.

_____ Then the agouti puts nuts in the ground to eat later.

_____ When the bees go to another flower, the pollen comes off their bodies.

_____ Consequently, new Brazil nut trees grow.

2. Use the sentences from Exercise 1 to complete the paragraph about the Brazil nut tree. Then answer the questions.

A Brazil nut tree in the Amazon rainforest can grow and produce nuts because of its ecosystem. When bees visit the flowers of the tree to eat, pollen gets on their bodies.

_____

_____

_____

1. Does the topic sentence show a cause or an effect?

2. Does the body of the paragraph show causes or effects? Check (✓) them.

3. What words or phrases helped you decide if the paragraph describes causes or effects? Circle them.

3. Work in small groups. Discuss the questions.

1. How are the Brazil nut tree, bees, and agouti connected in a web of life?

2. What does this web of life give to humans?

3. What might happen to this web if there were no bees or no agouti?

Global Listening

Organizing Information

Knowing how to organize information from a lecture is an important academic skill. This skill:

- helps you understand and remember the information you hear
- helps you find the relationships between ideas
- makes it easier for you to review information

One way to organize information is to use a **graphic organizer**. A graphic organizer is a chart or diagram that shows the organization of information. You can use graphic organizers to take notes on a lecture. You can also use them to organize your ideas for a paper or presentation.

---

[1] **agouti** _n_ a small tropical animal about the size of a rabbit

affect *v* to cause a change in someone or something

depend on *v* to need the help of someone or something

destroy *v* to break or damage completely; **destruction** *n*

disappear *v* to go away suddenly

in danger *adj* in a situation where something bad or harmful might happen

replace *v* to take someone from their job or something from its place, and put a new person or thing there

1. 🎧 *Listen to the lecture. Complete the graphic organizer with the information from the box that you will also hear. Then compare your graphic organizer with a partner's.*

farms and farm animals	homes	paper and building materials
food	medicine	rain forest

Web of Life—Rain Forest

CAUSE

Destruction of

_____

• Land used for

_____

• Trees used for

_____

EFFECTS

A lot of animals lose

_____

and

_____

Lost opportunity to find

_____

2. *Circle the correct answer to complete each statement.*

1. We are all connected in the web of life, _____.
   a. but people who live far away from the Amazon don't need to worry about it
   b. and people around the world depend on healthy rain forests

2. The professor uses the example of the bees and Brazil nut trees to show that _____.
   a. big things can depend on small things
   b. rain forest plants depend on pollination

3. There are many causes of rain forest destruction, _____.
   a. and humans are responsible for many of them
   b. but the rain forest is not in danger

4. One effect of rain forest destruction is _____.
   a. more bees that pollinate plants
   b. the loss of new medicines

5. The professor believes that the health of people is _____.
   a. connected to the health of the rain forests
   b. more important than the health of the rain forests

Focused Listening

1. ⌒ *Listen to the lecture again. Circle the correct answer to complete each sentence.*

Example

Fifty to seventy / (*Seventy to ninety*) percent of all plants in the rain forest depend on pollination.

1. The Brazil nut business is worth *50 million / 5 million* U.S. dollars a year.

2. Today in the Amazon, rain forest is destroyed to *build new houses / use for farms.*

3. *Twenty percent / Two percent* of the Amazon rain forest has been destroyed.

4. *Many / Few* of our medicines come from rain forest plants.

5. Scientists have tested only *10 percent / one percent* of the plants from the rain forest to use for medicines.

Listening for Cause-and-Effect Expressions

Speakers use these expressions to introduce causes:
   because (of), since, due to
Example

                                cause
Farmers sell their rain forest land **because** they need money.

Speakers use these expressions to introduce effects:
   therefore, consequently, so, as a result
Example

                                 effect
Farmers need money. **Therefore**, they sell their rain forest land.

As you listen to a lecture, notice these expressions.

2. Listen to the excerpts from the lecture. Circle the cause-and-effect expression you hear.

🎧 **Excerpt One**

since   consequently

🎧 **Excerpt Two**

so   since

🎧 **Excerpt Three**

therefore   since

3. 🎧 Listen to the excerpt from the lecture. Complete the excerpt with the cause-and-effect expressions you hear.

Unfortunately, the web of life of the Amazon is in danger. In fact, 20 percent of the rain forest has disappeared, (1) _____ human actions. Local people and international companies are burning forests down to use the land for farms and farm animals. In addition, people around the world use paper and building materials made from millions of rain forest trees. These actions have serious effects on all living things.

First, (2) _____ trees are disappearing, many animals are losing their homes and food. A lot of them die. (3) _____ many living things depend on each other, when some die, the whole web of life is affected.

4. Discuss the questions in small groups. Then share your ideas with the class.

1. According to the lecture, how are people connected to the rain forest? What other ways can you think of? Make a list in your notebook.

2. According to the lecture, how are people destroying the rain forest? What other reasons can you think of? Make a list in your notebook.

3. Which statement would the professor agree with? Which statement do you agree with? Explain your answers.
   - People should stop rain forest destruction; we need to protect planet Earth.
   - People should use the rain forest however they wish because they need to support their families.

Checkpoint 1   PEARSON LONGMAN myacademicconnectionslab

3

Building Academic Reading Skills

In this section, you will learn additional tools that effective writers use to organize cause-and-effect ideas.

For online assignments, go to

PEARSON LONGMAN
myacademicconnectionslab

For online assignments, go to

Key Words

benefit *n* something that helps you

cost *n* the amount of money you must pay in order to buy, do, or produce something; *v* to have a particular price; **costly** *adj*

degrade *v* to make something worse than it was; **degradation** *n;* **degraded** *adj*

economy *n* the way that money, business, and products are organized in a country or area; **economic** *adj*

process *n* a set of actions or events that cause change

valuable *adj* important; costing a lot of money; **value** *n, v*

worth *adj* having a particular value

Before You Read

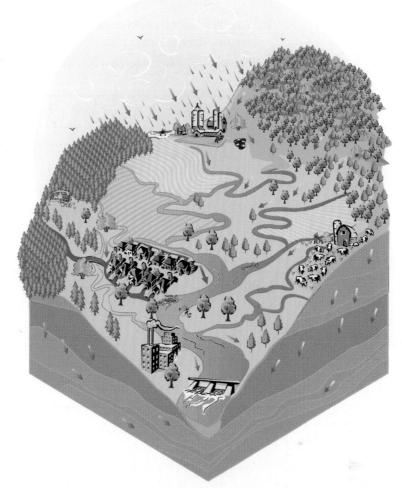

Ecosystems provide people with many important products and services. The watershed shown in this diagram is an ecosystem service. As water moves through the plants and land in a watershed, it becomes clean.

1. *Read the paragraph about water purification, an ecosystem service. Circle the correct words to complete the paragraph.*

Pure water is very (1) *valuable / degraded*. The (2) *cost / benefit* of clean water comes from healthy ecosystems around watersheds—places like forests, where water from rain travels before it goes into rivers or lakes. During the (3) *cost / process* of moving slowly through the watershed, water gets clean. Watersheds can become (4) *degraded / worth* when people build things like roads and parking lots in these areas. As a result, unclean water runs into rivers and lakes. This can have a big (5) *benefit / cost* for the environment and the (6) *economy / process*. For this reason, it is important to protect watersheds.

2. *Think about a natural place in your area. Read the questions and complete the chart with your examples. Then discuss the same questions with a partner and add your partner's examples to the chart.*

1. What is a natural ecosystem that you enjoy in your area? What services, or benefits, does this ecosystem bring to people or to the local economy?

2. How are these services valuable to you? Why?

Ecosystem	Service/Benefit	Value to You

Example
river by my house
	• *fun: swimming,
	  boating*
	• *water for the city*
	• *fish*
	• *beautiful and quiet*
		• *good for relaxing*
		• *less money than
		  going out*
		• *drinking water*
		• *cheap fish for
		  dinner, cheaper
		  than the market
		  and delicious!*

My example		
My partner's example		

Global Reading

Cause-and-Effect Organization: Block Organization

Cause and effect is a common organizational pattern for science texts. In block organization, all the causes are discussed together in one section, often in one paragraph, and all the effects are discussed in another block. (Note: Some texts discuss only causes or only effects.)

NATURE'S SERVICES: WHAT ARE THEY WORTH?

1   What is clean drinking water worth to you? How about good food? Ecosystems provide humans with many important things, including products like food and medicine and services such as air and water purification. These benefits are called *ecosystem services.*

2   Recently, human actions have caused costly degradation to some valuable ecosystem services. In the Catskill Mountains of New York State, watersheds were degraded due to the destruction of forests for farming and building. And in Brazil, because of rain forest destruction and the use of insecticides,[1] there are not enough insects to pollinate certain important food plants. These examples show us how our actions can be very costly to people and the economy.

3   Losing ecosystem services has serious effects on people's lives and health. When the Catskills watersheds became too small to purify water well, the drinking water in nearby New York City became unhealthy. In Brazil, destruction of the valuable ecosystem service of pollination caused the prices of fruits and vegetables to go higher. Since many people cannot buy the more expensive products, they buy cheaper, less healthy foods. This affects their health.

4   Destruction and degradation of ecosystem services also affect the economy, since fixing or replacing the services costs a lot of money. After the degradation of the Catskills watershed, the city of New York had two choices: First, the city could buy the watershed and protect it. Then the forests could make the water clean again. This would cost about a billion dollars. Second, the city could build a water purification plant. This would cost six to eight billion dollars to build and $300 million each year after that. Since

Pollinating plants by hand is very expensive.

building the water purification plant was much more expensive, the city decided to buy and protect the watershed. However, this was still a very costly solution for the city. In Brazil, the cost of losing pollination services has also been very high. Now many fruit plants must be pollinated by hand. This is expensive for farmers. It is also expensive for other people because it results in high food prices at the market.

5   Losing the ecosystem services the Earth provides would cause serious economic and health problems for everyone. Ecosystem services may be worth $33 trillion, and many economies on Earth would stop without them. (Costanza, et al., 1997) In addition, people's health would be seriously affected without these ecosystem services.

6   Clearly, ecosystem services are too valuable to lose.

---

[1] **insecticide** *n* a chemical used for killing insects

Costanza, R. et al. (1997). The value of the world's ecosystem services and natural capital. *Nature, 387*(May), 253–260.

2. *Complete the tasks. Discuss your answers with the class.*

1. Underline the main idea of the entire text.
2. Circle the cause-and-effect expressions.
3. How are the paragraphs in the body of the text (paragraphs 2–5) organized?
   - Paragraph _____ tells the causes of destruction to two ecosystem services.
   - Paragraph _____ discusses the effects on people's lives.
   - Paragraph _____ discusses the economic effects of this destruction.
   - Paragraph _____ tells the possible effects of losing all ecosystem services.
4. Did the use of cause-and-effect expressions help you to recognize the organization of ideas? If so, how?
5. Underline the concluding sentence of the entire text twice.

Focused Reading

1. *Read the text on page 29 again. Take notes on supporting details in the chart.*

Paragraph	Main Ideas	Details
Paragraph 1	Ecosystems provide many important _____ and _____.	• _____ • _____
Paragraph 2	causes of destruction: _____ _____	• Catskills _____ _____ • Brazil _____ _____
Paragraph 3	effects: people's lives and _____	• degradation of Catskills watershed: _____ _____ • less pollination in Brazil _____ _____

Paragraph	Main Ideas	Details
Paragraph 4	effects: _____	• Catskills _____ _____ • Brazil _____ _____
Paragraph 5	Losing ecosystem services: serious _____ _____	• _____ _____ • _____ _____

2. *Write short answers to the questions. Use your notes from the chart in Exercise 1.*

1. What are two ecosystem services described in the text? _____
_____
_____

2. What were two causes of destruction to the Catskills watershed? _____
_____
_____

3. Loss of pollination in Brazil has affected what kinds of food? _____
_____
_____

4. How much would it have cost New York City to build a water purification
plant? _____
_____
_____

5. How much are ecosystem services worth, according to the study by Robert
Costanza? _____
_____
_____

3. *Brainstorm with your class about ecosystems that are in danger. On your own, find information about another ecosystem. In your notebook, write at least two short answers for each question. Use cause-and-effect structure and expressions when possible.*

Examples

The ecosystem service of _____ provides _____.

The ecosystem is in danger due to _____.

1. What service(s) does this ecosystem provide?
2. What are the causes of degradation to this ecosystem?
3. What are the effects of this degradation?
4. Can humans stop the degradation and fix the ecosystem? If so, how? If not, can they replace the ecosystem?

Checkpoint 2 PEARSON LONGMAN myacademicconnectionslab

Before You Speak

Preparing for an Oral Presentation

In academic courses, students often give short presentations. When you speak, it is better to use notes rather than to read a paper word for word. That way, you can look at your audience while you talk. To prepare for your presentation, you can take notes on the introduction, main ideas, details, and conclusion in several ways:

- In an outline
- In a PowerPoint presentation
- On note cards

Practice giving your presentation with a clear, strong voice. Look up from your notes as much as possible.

1. ∩ *Listen to a student presentation. As you listen, complete the note cards on page 33 with the words from the box. Then compare notes with a partner's.*

costly	economy	pollination	work
diet	expensive	web of life	

4

Building Academic Speaking Skills

In this section, you will practice preparing oral presentations. Then you will prepare and give a presentation about the causes and/or effects of destruction to an ecosystem service. You will use ideas and vocabulary from this unit.

For online assignments, go to

PEARSON LONGMAN myacademicconnectionslab

A. Intro: Pollination and the loss of bees

1. Bees used for:

• honey

• _____ services

1. bees are leaving their beehives

2. smaller bee population= costly

consequences

B. Causes:

• too much _____

• poor _____

• insecticides used on farms

C. Effects:

• _____ food

• food not as good

• bad for the _____

D. Conclusion:

• bees are important to our

_____

• loss of bees: very _____

• need to find way to save bees

Key Words

honey *n* a sweet, sticky liquid made by bees and eaten by other animals and humans

population *n* the number of people or animals living in a certain area

2. *Work with a partner. Read the statements. Decide if they are true or false. Write* **T** *(true) or* **F** *(false).*

_____ a. Beekeepers use bees mainly to produce honey.

_____ b. Pollination services are very valuable.

_____ c. The bee population is growing.

_____ d. Bees may be disappearing because they work too hard.

_____ e. Pollination by people is not as good as pollination by bees.

_____ f. The speaker hopes scientists will soon find a way to improve pollination by humans.

Focused Speaking

You can use certain expressions to help your listeners follow your presentation.

To introduce your main idea or topic:

Today I am going to talk about . . .

My presentation today is on . . .

To introduce a point:

First/Second, . . .

Next, . . .

Another cause/effect is . . .

Finally, . . .

My final point is . . .

To conclude your presentation:

In conclusion, . . .

To close, . . .

To ask if there are any questions from your listeners:

Are there any questions?

Do you have any questions?

1. 🎧 *Listen again to the presentation in* Before You Speak *on page 32. Check (✓) the expressions you hear.*

_____ Today I am going to talk about . . .

_____ My presentation today is on . . .

_____ First, . . .

_____ Second, . . .

_____ Next, . . .

_____ Another cause is . . .

_____ Another effect is . . .

_____ Finally, . . .

_____ My final point, . . .

_____ In conclusion, . . .

_____ To close, . . .

_____ Are there any questions?

_____ Do you have any questions?

2. Complete the note cards to prepare a short presentation about causes and effects of degraded watersheds in the Catskill Mountains as described in the reading on page 29.

A. Introduction: Causes and effects of degraded watersheds in the Catskill Mountains	B. Causes:

C. Effects:	D. Conclusion:

3. Work with a partner. Take turns giving your presentations, using your note cards. Use the cause-and-effect words and expressions that you have studied in this unit, as well as the expressions in the skills box on page 34. Give feedback on your partner's presentation. Tell your partner one thing that he or she did well and one thing that he or she could do better.

Integrated Speaking Task

You have read about and listened to a lecture and a presentation about the web of life and ecosystem services. You will now use your knowledge of the unit content, topic vocabulary, cause-and-effect structure, and presentation techniques to plan and give a presentation about the cause(s) and/or effect(s) of the degradation of an ecosystem service.

Follow the steps to prepare your presentation.

Step 1: Choose an ecosystem to present. (You may use one of the ecosystems you discussed on pages 28 and 32.) Write notes in the chart to connect your topic to ideas from the reading and listenings. If needed, use the library or the Internet to find information.

Ecosystem: _____	Location: _____
Service(s) provided	
Causes of degradation / destruction	
Effects of destruction (health, economic, environmental, etc.)	
Related examples from this unit	

Step 2: Decide whether you will talk about causes, effects, or both. Then write notes on note cards.

Step 3: Practice the presentation with your note cards. Try speaking in front of a mirror and not reading from your notes word for word. Use the expressions you have learned to show cause and effect and to help your audience follow your ideas.

Step 4: Give your presentation in a small group. Answer your classmates' questions. As you listen to other students' presentations, take note of whether they discuss causes, effects, or both. Think of one question to ask each presenter.

UNIT

3

Stress and Health

Unit Description

Content: This course is designed to familiarize the student with the concept of stress and how it affects health. Students will also learn strategies for stress management.

Skills: Coherence and Cohesion

- Recognizing coherence in texts
- Using connectors for cohesion
- Using transition words for cohesion
- Listening for organization: Speech markers
- Listening for examples
- Planning a coherent paragraph
- Using cohesive expressions

Unit Requirements

Readings: "Understanding Stress" (an excerpt from a health management textbook)

"Stress in the Modern World: Technostress" (an excerpt from a website)

Lecture: "Stress Management"

Integrated Writing Task: Writing a coherent and cohesive paragraph about technostress

Assignments: www.MyAcademicConnectionsLab.com

1

Preview

For online assignments, go to

PEARSON LONGMAN
myacademicconnectionslab

Key Words

emotional *adj* related to feelings

manage *v* to succeed in doing something difficult, such as dealing with a problem

respond *v* to react to something that has been said or done

stress *n* the feeling of being worried because of difficulties in your life; **stressed** *adj*; **stressful** *adj*

stressor *n* a situation that causes a stress reaction

Previewing the Academic Content

Every day we experience different kinds of problems—some small, some big. For some people, getting to work might be the most difficult part of the day. Others experience real dangers to their physical and emotional happiness—an accident, the sickness of a loved one, or the loss of a job. Stress is how our bodies and minds respond to these situations. Stress is a normal part of life, but too much stress can seriously affect our health. Scientists and health professionals study how stress affects the human body, and they suggest ways to lower stress. They also study new kinds of stress that people are experiencing in today's world. You will examine these issues in this unit.

1. *Look at the pictures. Discuss the questions in small groups.*

1. What is the cause of stress in each picture?

2. What are some other common causes of stress?

3. Do you think life today is more or less stressful than life 50 years ago? How about life 5,000 years ago? Explain.

2. Look at the Student Stress Scale, which lists common stressors that students experience. Check (✓) each event you have experienced in the last two years.

THE STUDENT STRESS SCALE

✓	STRESSFUL EVENTS
	death of a close family member
	death of a close friend
	divorce of parents
	being very sick or getting hurt in an accident
	getting married
	losing a job
	failing an important class
	change in the health of a family member
	being pregnant or having a child
	being upset with a close friend
	change in money situation
	changing studies in school
	having trouble with parents
	having a new boyfriend or girlfriend
	taking more classes in school
	having success with an important task or event
	starting school or a new semester
	moving to a new place
	having a problem with a teacher

Adapted from Holmes, T., & Rahe, R.H. (1967). The social readjustment rating scale. *Journal of Psychosomatic Research, 11,* 213.

3. Discuss the questions in small groups.

1. How many events did you check? Do you think your overall stress level is high, medium, or low? Which member of your group has experienced the most stressful events?

2. Do any of the events on the list surprise you?

3. What other events do you think should be on the list?

4. What do you think causes more stress—big events (like those in the scale) or daily experiences (like losing your keys)?

Previewing the Academic Skills Focus

In this unit, you will learn how to recognize coherence and cohesion in readings and lectures. You will also learn how to create coherence and cohesion in your own writing.

Coherence and Cohesion

A text has **coherence** when all of the ideas are related to the main idea of the text. **Cohesion** is the use of words and expressions to connect ideas within and between sentences. Understanding coherence and cohesion will help you to follow readings and lectures and to write more effectively.

1. Read the two paragraphs about stress. Notice how they are different.

Paragraph A

Some experts think that the best way to find out a student's stress level is to look at the small daily stressors in his/her life. Some examples of daily stresses are arriving late to class, losing a car key, and having problems with a roommate. According to Blonna (2005), these daily stresses can tell us more about a person's stress level than big events can. Big life events can give a *general* idea about a person's stress level. However, they are hard to measure.[1] In addition, Miller and Rahe (1997) found that people in today's world respond differently to big life events than people did in the past. For example, getting a traffic ticket was not a big cause of stress 30 years ago, but today a ticket might cost a lot of money. This may cause a person to experience much more stress.

---

[1] **measure** *v* to find out the size, weight, or amount of something

Blonna, R. (2005). *Coping with stress in a changing world.* New York: McGraw-Hill.
Miller, M.A., & Rahe, R.H. (1997). Life changes scaling for the 1990s. *Journal of Psychosomatic Research, 43,* 279–292.

Paragraph B

Some experts think that the best way to find out a student's stress level is to look at the small daily stressors in her life. Like losing keys and having problems with roommates. My sister often fights with her boyfriend, too. This causes a lot of stress in her life. Blonna points out that these daily stresses can tell us more about a person's stress level than big events can. Big life events can give a *general* idea about a person's stress level. You can't measure them easily. Miller and Rahe found that people in today's world respond differently to big life events today than they did in the past. Getting a traffic ticket was not a big cause for stress 30 years ago. Today a traffic ticket might be very expensive. Last week I got a ticket for driving too fast.

2. *Complete the tasks and discuss the questions in small groups.*

1. Underline the topic sentence of each paragraph. Which paragraph supports its main idea more clearly?

2. Are there any sentences that don't relate to or support the main idea in the less coherent paragraph? Draw a line through them.

3. Circle the words and expressions that help connect the sentences in the coherent paragraph.

Before You Read

Recognizing Coherence in Texts

Coherence makes a text easy to understand. In a coherent text:
- All ideas support the main idea of the text.
- Every paragraph discusses only one main idea.
- The connection between ideas is clear.
- The organization and order of ideas is logical.

1. *You will read a textbook passage with this main idea:* **Modern life has created serious problems related to stress**. *Check (✓) the ideas that you think will be in the passage.*

_____ Many things cause stress in today's world.

_____ Stress can make people very sick.

_____ Students should take breaks when studying for a test.

_____ Problems with money cause a lot of stress today.

_____ People in Tokyo have busy lives.

_____ People live longer now than they did in the past.

2. Compare answers on page 41 with a partner's. Explain how the ideas you checked are related to the main idea.

3. Discuss the questions with your partner.

1. Has stress ever caused you to do poorly at your work? Explain.

2. Has stress ever helped you (or someone you know) to do good work? Explain.

3. Has stress ever caused you (or someone you know) any health problems? Explain.

Global Reading

1. Look at the pictures. Discuss the questions in small groups.

1. What causes stress for the people in the pictures?

2. How is stress different for each person? Explain.

2. Read the textbook excerpt. Take notes on the main ideas.

Key Words

lifestyle *n* the way in which you live, including your job, what you own, and what you do

release *v* to let someone or something go free

Understanding Stress

1 Stress—the way a person responds to changes and difficult situations—is a common experience that people all over the world share (Blonna, 2005). In fact, most people have stressful experiences every day. However, research shows that people experience more stress today than they did in the past. Forty-eight percent of people in the United States report that they feel more stressed today than they did five years ago.[1] In addition, most doctor visits in the world (three out of five) happen because of problems related to stress.[2] Scientists and health workers are interested in

[1] APA survey, 2007
[2] Foundation for Integrated Research in Mental Health, 2007

this subject because high stress levels have serious consequences that can affect people's health and daily lives.

2 Researchers at Rutgers University suggest that recent changes in people's lifestyles have caused more stress. Stress causes the body to experience physical changes such as a faster heartbeat and breathing rate. The right level of stress can make a person feel stronger and more energetic. Researchers believe that in the past this energy helped people to hunt for animals and to protect themselves from danger (Cannon, 1932). They released stress with physical activity involved in hunting, and then their bodies could relax again. Although people today still experience an increase in energy in response to stress, they do not use energy like the hunter-gatherers[3] did. As a result, it is more difficult for their bodies to let go of stress.

3 Too much stress—or stress that continues for a long time—can cause serious physical and emotional problems. These problems include trouble sleeping, sickness, and pain. Heart disease and even cancer probably result from stress. Moreover, people under stress are in more danger of having an accident at work or while driving, and they might start bad habits more easily such as smoking or eating too much.

4 It is important to point out that stress is not always bad, however. Actually, today's busy lifestyles cause two kinds of stress—eustress and distress. Eustress is the effect of positive events that cause a change in a person's life. Eustress provides the amount of stress that is just right for a person to grow, to stay energetic, and to feel happy with life. For instance, getting married is a happy life event for most people. However, getting married is also a big change, so it causes stress. Distress, on the other hand, is the effect of bad or difficult experiences. Problems with money, school, or relationships are common causes of distress in modern life. According to the Holmes and Rahe Social Readjustment Rating Scale (1967), the death of a husband, wife, or child causes the most distress in a person's life. Distress can cause serious health and emotional problems, but eustress can actually improve a person's well-being.

---

[3] **hunter-gatherer** *n* a member of a group of people who live by hunting and looking for plants to eat, rather than by keeping animals for food or growing crops

Blonna, R. (2005). *Coping with stress in a changing world.* New York: McGraw-Hill.

Cannon, W. (1932). *The wisdom of the body.* London: Kegan Paul, Trench, Trubner.

Holmes, T., & Rahe, R.H. (1967). The social readjustment rating scale. *Journal of Psychosomatic Research, 11,* 213.

3. Circle the letter of the sentence that best expresses the main idea of each paragraph. Use your notes.

Paragraph 1

    a. More stress has become a problem in modern life.

    b. Stress is common all over the world.

    c. Stress makes people unhealthy.

Paragraph 2

    a. Stress helped hunter-gatherers hunt and protect themselves.

    b. Changes in lifestyle have caused more problems with stress.

    c. People today use less energy than people in the past.

(continued on next page)

Paragraph 3

    a. Too much stress causes serious physical and emotional problems.

    b. Trouble sleeping is one effect of stress.

    c. Stress causes changes in the body.

Paragraph 4

    a. Good stress is called eustress.

    b. Bad stress is called distress.

    c. Stress can be good or bad.

Using Connectors for Cohesion

Connectors are words and expressions that connect two ideas in a sentence or combine two sentences. Use *and* to connect ideas or to combine sentences that are similar or that give extra information. Use *but* to connect ideas or to combine sentences that are contrasting or opposite.

Connecting ideas

I need to study. I need to finish my paper. → I need to study *and* finish my paper.

My job is interesting. My job is stressful. → My job is interesting *but* stressful.

Combining sentences

I have too much stress. My family doesn't help. → I have too much stress, *and* my family doesn't help.

I don't have enough money. I feel fine. → I don't have enough money, *but* I feel fine.

To combine two complete sentences, use a comma before *and* or *but*. Do not use a comma to connect two ideas in the same sentence.

4. *Write* and *or* but *to connect the ideas as one sentence.*

    1. I left my house early. I arrived at work late.

    _____

    2. Hunter-gatherers hunted. They looked for plants.

    _____

    3. Getting married is exciting. It is stressful.

    _____

5. *Use* and *or* but *to combine the sentences.*

    1. Stress can give people energy at first. It is usually not a problem if they can release the energy.

    _____

2. Distress can cause physical problems. Eustress can help you grow.

_____

3. People in the past used a lot of energy. People today do fewer physical activities.

_____

Focused Reading

1. *Read the textbook passage on pages 42–43 again. Complete the chart with the missing information. If the information isn't in the text, leave the chart blank. Compare your chart with a partner's.*

Key Point	Definition	Explanation or Examples from Text
Stress	response of a person's mind and body to a change or difficult situation	• getting married • death of husband, wife, or child • problems with money, school, or family
Changes in lifestyle		
Consequences of stress		
Eustress		
Distress		

2. *Circle the correct answer to complete each statement. Use your notes to help you.*

1. Most people experience stressful events every *day / week*.

2. In paragraph 1, the author gives statistics about stress because *they are entertaining to the reader / they show why experts are interested in stress*.

3. Stress can make people feel *relaxed / stronger*.

4. The author discusses hunter-gatherers to show *that they were not stressed / how our response to stress has changed over time*.

5. *A problem in school / Getting married* is an example of a positive stressful life experience.

6. According to Holmes, *divorce / marriage* is more stressful.

Using Transition Words for Cohesion

Transition words and phrases create cohesion by showing the relationship between ideas in paragraphs. They are often at the beginning of a sentence and followed by a comma.

• To add information about or build on ideas from the previous sentence, use:
   Also, In addition, . . . or *Moreover, . . .*
These terms are similar in meaning to the word *and*.

Examples

I am stressed. I get upset with people. *In addition*, I worry about my family.
Also, I am worried about finding a job.
I have to study for an exam. *Moreover*, I have to finish a paper tonight.

• To contrast information, use: *However, . . .* or *On the other hand, . . .*
These terms are similar in meaning to *but*.

Examples

My friends want me to help them with their problems. *However*, I have no time.
My housemate is very friendly. *On the other hand*, he always makes a big mess.

Use these transition words at the beginning of a sentence. Do not use them after a comma.

Right: Many women are stressed. *However*, working mothers are the most stressed.
Wrong: Many women are stressed, *however*, working mothers are the most stressed.

3. *Read* Understanding Stress *on pages 42–43 again. Circle the transition words.*

4. Complete the chart. Answer the questions about yourself in the Me column. Then ask a partner the questions and complete the My Partner column.

	Me	My Partner
What causes the most distress in your life?		
What causes eustress in your life?		
What, if any, health or emotional problems do you experience because of stress?		

5. Write three sentences comparing and contrasting you and your partner. Use transition words and phrases where possible. Then share one sentence with the class.

Example

Homework causes both of us distress. In addition, we both feel distress from worrying too much.

Stress causes sleep problems for my partner. However, I always sleep well.

_____

_____

_____

Building Academic Listening Skills

In this section, you will learn more about the tools that effective speakers use to create coherence and cohesion. For online assignments, go to

myacademicconnectionslab

Key Words

anxiety *n* a feeling of worry; **anxious** *adj*

realize *v* to know or understand something that you did not know before

schedule *n* a plan of what you will do and when you will do it

technique *n* a special way of doing something

Before You Listen

1. *Complete each statement with a correct key word.*

1. Is it already 4:00 P.M.? I didn't _____ it was that late.

2. I'm making a _____ for next week. I'm going to study every evening from 7:00 to 9:00 P.M.

3. Exercise is my favorite _____ for lowering stress. It makes me feel great.

4. The presentation I'm giving next week is causing me a lot of _____. I'm afraid I won't do well.

2. *Complete the questionnaire from a student health office. You will use the bottom portion of the questionnaire later.*

Student Stress Questionnaire

How often do you use these stress management techniques?
Check (✓) **Always**, **Sometimes**, or **Never**.

Stress Management Technique	Always	Sometimes	Never
I make a schedule to manage my time.	❏	❏	❏
I take time to relax and have fun.	❏	❏	❏
I say "no" if I am too busy to do something.	❏	❏	❏
I sleep eight or more hours a night.	❏	❏	❏
I exercise three or more times a week.	❏	❏	❏
I do one thing at a time.	❏	❏	❏
I arrive early for appointments.	❏	❏	❏
_____	❏	❏	❏
_____	❏	❏	❏
_____	❏	❏	❏

Remember: Taking time to manage stress will keep you healthy and happy!

3. *Work in small groups. Compare your answers to the questionnaire. Then discuss the questions.*

1. What other techniques do you use to manage stress? Add three of your own or your classmates' ideas to the questionnaire, and check the correct column.

2. Do you use different management techniques for different stressors? Explain.

3. What is your biggest stressor in life, and which technique would be best for managing it?

Global Listening

Listening for Organization: Speech Markers

In Unit 2 you learned special words and phrases to show the introduction, main ideas, and conclusion of a presentation. These expressions are called **speech markers**. Listening for speech markers will help you follow presentations and lectures and understand how they are organized.

<u>Introduction</u>

Today I'd like to talk about . . .

Today's topic is . . .

The focus of today's lecture is . . .

<u>Main Idea</u>

The first/second/next/last point I'd like to make . . .

This brings us to another point I'd like to make . . .

Finally, . . .

<u>Conclusion</u>

To sum up today's lecture, . . .

In conclusion, . . .

1. ◠ *Listen to the beginning of a presentation by a counselor from a campus health services office. Check (✓) the answers.*

1. What is the main idea of the presentation?

   _____ Stress has many consequences.

   _____ Many students are stressed.

   _____ There are ways to lower stress.

2. What expression does the presenter use to introduce the main idea?

   _____ The topic today is . . .

   _____ Today I will talk to you about . . .

   _____ The focus of the presentation is . . .

2. 🎧 *Listen to the entire presentation. Complete the middle column of the chart with the main ideas in the box. Listen again and write the speech markers used to introduce each main idea. Compare your chart with a partner's.*

Learn to use your time better.

Learn what causes you stress and change how you respond to that situation.

Having a healthy lifestyle helps you manage stress.

~~There are ways you can lower your stress.~~

Manage your stress to live a healthy life.

Part of Lecture	Main Ideas	Speech Markers
Introduction	*There are ways you can lower your stress.*	*Today I will talk to you about . . .*
Part 1		
Part 2		
Part 3		
Conclusion		

3. *Read the statements. Decide if they are true or false. Write **T** (true) or **F** (false).*

_____ 1. In stress inoculation, you do not think about the cause of stress.

_____ 2. Time management helps students do better in school.

_____ 3. People who manage their time well have no time to relax.

_____ 4. Staying healthy helps you manage stress better.

Focused Listening

Listening for Examples

There are other speech markers that speakers use to introduce examples and to create cohesion:

For example, . . .
One example of . . . is
Another example is . . .
For instance, . . .
To illustrate, . . .
. . . such as . . .
. . . like . . .

Pay attention to these speech markers as you listen to lectures. They show that an example follows.

1. ∩ *Listen to the presentation again. Note the expressions the speaker uses to introduce examples. Then take notes on the examples in the* Lecture Examples *column. Compare your chart with a partner's. You will complete the* My Examples *column later.*

Techniques	Expressions Used	Lecture Examples	My Examples
Inoculation	For example,	Speaking in public: prepare for the stressful event	

(continued on next page)

Techniques	Expressions Used	Lecture Examples	My Examples
Time management			
Healthy lifestyle			

2. *How could you use each technique in your life? Write examples in the My Examples column. Then share your ideas with a partner.*

3. *Listen to the excerpts from the presentation. Circle the best word to complete each statement.*

⌒ Excerpt One

The presenter believes that speaking in public is a(n) ***common / uncommon*** fear.

⌒ Excerpt Two

The presenter suggests that most people think those who schedule their time are usually too ***stressed / busy*** to relax.

⌒ Excerpt Three

The presenter ***thinks / does not think*** that people with a healthy lifestyle have no stress.

4. *Prepare a one- to two-minute presentation on your experience with stress. Follow the steps.*

Step 1: Choose one of the topics from the list or choose your own topic.
- A health problem related to stress
- How eustress helps you do well
- How people in your culture manage stress
- Why college students today have more stress

Step 2: Write the main idea about the topic in the outline on page 53. Then add three supporting details and a conclusion. Try to make a connection to at least one idea from the reading and one idea from the listening.

(Main idea) _____

_____

(Details)

- _____

_____

- _____

_____

- _____

_____

(Conclusion) _____

Step 3: Practice your presentation. Use connectors and speech markers to add cohesion.

Step 4: Give your presentation in a small group.

Example

Last semester, I didn't take care of my health because of stress. For instance, in the last two weeks of class, I stayed up late every night to finish my assignments. In addition, I drank a lot of coffee to stay awake, and then I couldn't sleep. Also, I ate a lot of unhealthy food, such as pizza and cookies. This caused me many health problems.

| Checkpoint 2 | PEARSON LONGMAN myacademicconnectionslab |

Before You Write

Planning a Coherent Paragraph

You can use the outlining skills you learned in Unit 1 to plan a paragraph. Following these guidelines will help you outline a coherent paragraph that is easy for readers to understand:

- **Topic Sentence:** Make sure that your main idea is clearly introduced in a topic sentence.
- **Body:** Every detail should relate to and support your main idea. In addition, make sure that your ideas are in a logical order. Use cohesive expressions to show organization and to introduce details and examples. Use connectors and transitions to connect ideas and sentences.
- **Concluding sentence:** Often, a concluding sentence repeats the main idea in different words or gives a final comment.

4

Building Academic Writing Skills

In this section, you will practice coherence and cohesion in writing. Then you will write a paragraph about stress. To write your paragraph, you will use ideas and vocabulary from this unit. For online assignments, go to

PEARSON LONGMAN
myacademicconnectionslab

1. *Read the two paragraph outlines. Discuss the questions with a partner.*

1. Does each outline include a topic sentence, body, and concluding sentence?
2. Does the topic sentence clearly state the main idea?
3. Do all the body details support the main idea? Are they in a logical order?
4. Does the concluding sentence relate to the main idea?
5. Which outline is better? Why?

Outline 1

Topic Sentence: Money is a big stressor for students.

Body/Details: • Jobs do not pay well.

• Schools are expensive—students borrow money.

• Cost of living is high—gas, food, rent.

• Need to buy expensive things—cars, computers, etc.

Concluding Sentence: In conclusion, today's students experience stress because of problems with money.

Outline 2

Topic Sentence: Jobs do not pay well.

Body/Details: • Schools are more expensive—students borrow money.

• Students have financial stress.

• Cost of living is high—gas, food, rent

• Money is a serious stressor for students.

Concluding Sentence: Finally, students need to buy cars and computers.

2. Read the paragraph. Is it coherent? Which outline from Exercise 1 does it follow?

Money is a big stressor for students. In today's world, many students have jobs. However, their jobs do not pay enough to cover all their costs. In addition, schools are more expensive these days than they were in the past, so many students must borrow money to pay for their school. The cost of living is also higher. For example, gas, food, and rent all cost more than they did in the past. Finally, many students must buy cars to get to school and computers to do their schoolwork. As a result, students often need more money than they have. In conclusion, today's students experience stress because of problems with money.

Focused Writing

Using Cohesive Expressions

Review the cohesive expressions you can use to help readers follow your paragraph.

To . . .	Use . . .
• add information and contrast	• *and, in addition, also, moreover* • *but, however, on the other hand*
• give examples	• *for example, for instance, to illustrate this, another example, such as, like*
• show order	• *first, second, next, last, finally*
• finish a paragraph	• *in conclusion, in summary*

1. Work with a partner. Complete the tasks.

1. Technostress is a feeling of anxiety caused by working with technology. Read the website article on page 56 about Patrick Ngo, a student who experiences technostress. Complete the article with cohesive expressions from the skill box on this page. More than one answer may be correct.

Stress in the Modern World: Technostress

WHAT'S
TECHNOSTRESS?

ARE YOU A
VICTIM?

REAL-LIFE
STORIES

GET HELP

SHARE YOUR
STORY

CONTACT US

Eighty-five percent of people have problems working with technology. Technostress is a common type of stress in today's world. Technostress is stress caused by technology, (1) _____ cell phones and computers. Technology can make a person's life easier (2) _____ more exciting. (3) _____, as Patrick Ngo found, it can also cause frustration.

Patrick, a Chinese student at the University of Bristol, likes to play computer games in his free time. He finds them challenging (4) _____ fun to play, (5) _____ they cause him a lot of stress when he doesn't win. (6) _____, he often spends too much time playing them, which has caused his studies and health to suffer. In many ways, the computer games are like the exciting hunt of the hunter-gatherers of the past. (7) _____, they get Patrick's energy going. (8) _____, unlike the hunter-gatherers, there is no release of stress. As a result, Patrick began to experience headaches and sleeping problems. After a visit to his university health center, Patrick now plays games less and exercises three times a week to control his technostress.

2. Underline the definition of technostress in the article.

3. Complete the chart on page 57 with information from the article.

4. Work in small groups. Make a list of other examples of technostress.

	Patrick's Case
Type of technostress	
Eustress / distress it causes	
Consequences of stress	
Stress management solutions	

2. *Follow the steps to write a short paragraph answering this question:* **How does Patrick Ngo's experience with technostress show the ideas about modern stress and stress management in this unit?** *Follow the steps.*

Step 1: Review the chart in Exercise 1. Add any new information related to the question.

Step 2: Make an outline to organize your ideas. Use the skill box on page 53 to check your outline.

Step 3: Write your paragraph. Remember to use cohesive expressions, connectors, and transitions.

Step 4: Work with a partner. Exchange paragraphs. Use the information in the skill box on page 53 to provide feedback on your partner's paragraph.

Integrated Writing Task

You have listened to a lecture and read texts about stress, stress management, and technostress. You will now use your knowledge of the unit content, topic vocabulary, and strategies for creating cohesion and coherence to write a paragraph on this topic: **What is one type of technostress you experience in your daily life? Explain the stress, describe its effects, and discuss ways you can try to manage it. Connect your experience to Patrick Ngo's experience with technostress.**

Follow the steps to write your paragraph.

Step 1: Complete the chart on page 58 with information about technostress in your life.

	Technostress in My Life
Type of technostress	
Eustress / Distress it causes	
Consequences of stress	
Stress management solutions	
How similar to / different from Patrick Ngo's experience?	

Step 2: Make a paragraph outline using ideas from the chart. Use the skill box on page 53 to check your outline.

Step 3: Write your paragraph on a separate piece of paper. Use your outline and the checklist in Step 4 to help you.

Step 4: Exchange paragraphs with a partner. Read your partner's paragraph and provide feedback. Use the checklist.

Paragraph Checklist	Yes	No
Does the paragraph have a clear topic sentence that introduces the main idea?		
Does the paragraph have details (ideas and examples) that relate to and support the main idea?		
Are the supporting details and examples in logical order?		
Does the paragraph have connectors and transitions that connect ideas and sentences and introduce details and examples?		
Does the paragraph have a concluding sentence that connects to the main idea?		

Step 5: Revise your paragraph based on your partner's feedback. Then share your paragraph in small groups.

UNIT 4
Literature
Folktales

Unit Description

Content: This course is designed to familiarize the student with the literary form of folktales.

Skills: Summarizing

- Recognizing summary statements
- Distinguishing major from minor points
- Using time-order words
- Paraphrasing
- Preparing narrative summaries
- Giving a narrative summary

Unit Requirements

Lecture: "Common Characteristics of Folktales"

Readings: *How Raven Gave Light* (a folktale)
"The Trickster" (a descriptive paragraph)
How Anansi Gave People Stories (a folktale)

Listening: *The Tree with the Golden Apples* (a narrative summary)

Integrated Speaking Task: Preparing and presenting an oral summary of a folktale

Assignments:
www.MyAcademicConnectionsLab.com

Preview

For online assignments, go to

Previewing the Academic Content

Many cultures, especially those that don't use writing, tell stories to explain the world and to pass down history and beliefs to the next generation. People have shared these stories, called folktales, in the oral tradition for hundreds or even thousands of years. Now the stories can be found in books, stories for children, and movies. Folktales have many purposes. Some teach lessons about life. Others explain mysterious events as being the results of magic. And some entertain the audience. In this unit, you will read and listen to folktales and learn about the common features of folktales.

1. ⌒ *Read and listen to an example of a short folktale,* How Raven Gave Light. *This folktale is popular in Alaska and in the Pacific Northwest area of the United States. It is about a time when people lived in darkness, and it explains how a bird named Raven gave people light.*

Key Words

character *n* a person in a book, story, movie etc.

culture *n* the beliefs, customs, and way of life of a society

feature *n* one part of something that people often notice because it is important or interesting

generation *n* all the people who are about the same age

magic *n* a special power used for making strange things happen; **magical** *adj*

oral *adj* spoken, not written

tradition *n* a belief or custom that has existed for a long time; **traditional** *adj*

HOW RAVEN GAVE LIGHT
As told by Marilyn Whirlwind (adapted)

A long time ago, Raven looked down from the sky. He saw that the people of the world were living in the dark because an old, selfish[1] chief [2] was hiding the great ball of light. Raven thought that people should not live in the dark, so he decided to bring light to them. The next day he used magic to change himself into a small leaf[3] from a tree and fell into a river. Soon after that, the chief's daughter came to the river for a drink of water. She drank the leaf, and the leaf grew in the young woman as a baby boy. When the baby was born, all loved him, especially the chief. But soon, the baby started to cry. He wanted to play with his grandfather's ball of light. The family could not make him stop crying for the ball. Finally, the chief gave the ball of light to the baby. As soon as he had the light, the baby changed back into Raven. He immediately threw the ball of light into the sky, so there was light everywhere! From then on, people lived in the light.

---

[1] **selfish** *adj* caring only about yourself and not other people
[2] **chief** *n* the leader of a group or tribe
[3] **leaf** *n* a flat, green part of a plant or tree that grows out of branches or a stem

2. Work with a partner. Complete the chart with information about the story.

When does the story happen?	*a long time ago*
Where does it happen?	
Who are the main characters?	
What is the problem?	
How is the problem solved?	

3. Discuss the questions in small groups.

1. Have you ever heard this folktale before? If so, was that story similar to the one you have just read or different? How?

2. What other folktales have you heard?

3. What kinds of stories did you hear as a child? Have you ever seen one of these stories written down or in a movie? If so, was the written story different from the one you heard?

This unit will help you recognize summaries in readings and lectures. You will also learn how to summarize material you read and hear.

Previewing the Academic Skills Focus

Summarizing

A **summary** briefly gives the main information of a longer written or spoken text in your own words. A good summary:
- includes the main points of the text
- answers important questions about the text (such as *Who?*, *What?*, *When?*, *Where?*, *Why?*, and *How?*)

A good summary does not:
- include unimportant details
- give your opinion

Summarizing what you read and hear in class can help you to review and understand the main ideas.

1. *Read the summaries of* How Raven Gave Light.

Summary 1

How Raven Gave Light is a very old Alaskan folktale. Long ago Raven saw that the people lived in darkness because a chief was hiding the ball of light in the sky. Raven wanted to help the people. First, he used magic to change into a baby boy, the chief's grandson. Then the baby cried for the ball of light until the chief finally gave it to him. Raven put the ball of light in the sky so the people could live in light.

Summary 2

Raven came down from the sky and saw that the people needed light because they were living in the dark. An old chief wanted to keep the light because he was selfish. Raven changed into a leaf and went into some water. Then Raven changed into a baby. Everybody loved the baby, but he cried because he wanted to play with the ball of light. The chief was tired of the crying, so he gave the baby the ball of light. This story was very interesting.

---

2. *Check (✓) the correct columns to complete the chart. Then compare answers in small groups. Which summary do you think is better? Explain.*

Which summary . . . ?	Summary 1	Summary 2
includes the main points of the text		
answers the question *When does the story happen?*		
answers the question *Where does the story happen?*		
answers the question *Who are the main characters?*		
answers the question *What is the problem?*		
answers the question *How is the problem solved?*		
includes unimportant details		
includes the writer's opinion		

2

Building Academic Listening Skills

In this section, you will learn more about how to recognize summary statements in a text. You will also learn how to recognize the ideas that are most important to include in a summary. For online assignments, go to

myacademicconnectionslab
PEARSON LONGMAN

Key Words

characteristic *n* a typical quality or feature of something or someone

clever *adj* able to use your intelligence to get what you want, sometimes in a slightly dishonest way

extraordinary *adj* very unusual, special, or surprising

role *n* the position or job that someone has in a group

task *n* a job or piece of work

Before You Listen

Circle the elements that you think make a good story. Then discuss your choices in small groups. Give examples from stories you like.

characters that seem real	humor (funny)	simple story
clever characters	interesting setting (place and time)	surprises
complex story		teaches a lesson
fight between good and bad	lots of action	other: _____
	magic	
happy ending	romance	

Global Listening

Recognizing Summary Statements

A **summary statement** is one sentence that brings together the most important ideas from a paragraph or a longer text. Summary statements are most often located in the conclusion of a paragraph, lecture, or text. In a longer text or lecture, each section or paragraph may have a summary statement. These expressions introduce summary statements:

> In conclusion, . . .
> To conclude, . . .
> In summary, . . .
> To sum it up, . . .

Recognizing summary statements will help you identify the main points of a reading or lecture.

1. 🎧 *Listen to the lecture. Pay attention to summary statements to help you identify the main ideas. Take notes on the main ideas in your notebook.*

2. *Check (✓) the three main ideas in the lecture. Use your notes to help you.*

_____ Storytellers from different cultures make changes to folktales.

_____ Folktales were not written down, so they changed over time.

_____ Animal characters in folktales have human-like qualities such as the ability to talk.

_____ Folktale characters are often simple.

_____ The plot of the story starts with a problem.

_____ The plot of the story is interesting.

3. 🎧 *Listen to the summary statement of the entire lecture to check your answers to Exercise 2. Circle the expression you hear.*

a. *In conclusion*   b. *In summary*   c. *To sum it up*

Focused Listening

1. 🎧 *Listen to the lecture again. Complete the outline using the words from the box. Then compare your outline with a partner's and make any necessary changes.*

characteristics	extraordinary	magic	task
clever	human	plot	traditions

Lecture Topic: Common (1) _____ of folktales

Oral tradition = stories changed based on:

  • storytellers' place

  • storytellers' (2) _____ and culture

Example: Raven = another animal in other stories

Similar characters

  • ordinary characters do (3) _____ things

  • have one or two strong characteristics

Examples: chief = selfish, not smart; Raven = generous,

(4) _____

  • animals with (5) _____ qualities

Examples: spider, turtle

Exciting plot

  • happens "a long time ago"

  • begins quickly with a problem

  • characters use tricks, skills, or (6) _____

    to complete a (7) _____

  • good characters win & bad characters lose

Conclusion: Common features of folktales

  • oral tradition

  • similar characters

  • strong (8) _____

Major points are main ideas and important details that are necessary for understanding. A good summary includes only major points. **Minor points** add interest or give extra information, such as examples, but they are not essential for understanding. Minor points are not included in a summary.

To find major points, ask yourself these questions:

- *Is this information important to understanding the text or lecture?*
- *Does this information give the main idea?*
- *Is this an important detail for understanding the main idea?*

To recognize minor points, ask yourself these questions:

- *If I take out this detail, can I still understand the text and the main idea?*
- *Is this a small detail? Does it only give extra information?*

2. *Review the outline in Exercise 1 on page 64. Put a* ***** *next to the major points— the main ideas and important details. Put an* ***X*** *next to the unimportant, minor details. Use the information in the skill box to help you decide. Compare your choices as a class and make any necessary changes.*

3. *Work with a partner. Summarize the lecture. Follow the steps.*

1. Review the skill box on page 61.

2. Make a list of the major points of the lecture. Leave out minor points.

3. Take turns summarizing the lecture. Use these expressions:
   - *The lecture was about . . .*
   - *The first/second/last point . . .*
   - *An important example of this . . .*

4. *Think of a folktale you know. Use the questions listed to help you organize information. Then tell your folktale to a partner.*

- What is the name of your folktale?

  _____

- When and where does the story happen?

  _____

  _____

- Who are the main characters?

  _____

  _____

- What is the problem and how is it solved?

  _____

  _____

5. *Work with a partner. Use the Venn diagram to compare and contrast your folktales. For example, compare time, place, characters, problems, and endings. Then use your Venn diagram to explain one similarity or difference to your class.*

Example

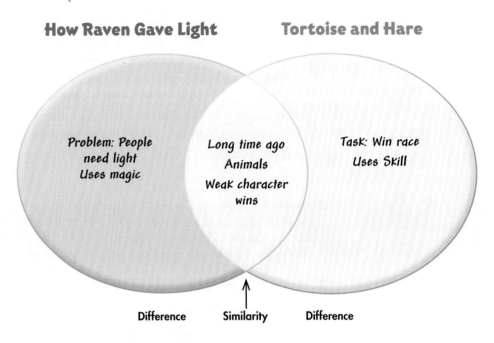

How Raven Gave Light   Tortoise and Hare

Problem: People
need light
Uses magic

Long time ago
Animals
Weak character
wins

Task: Win race
Uses Skill

Difference   **Similarity**   **Difference**

Title: _____   Title: _____

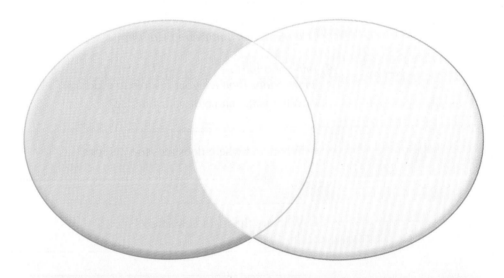

**Building
Academic
Reading Skills**

In this section, you
will learn about
paraphrasing, an
important academic
skill.

For online assignments,
go to

PEARSON LONGMAN
myacademicconnectionslab

Key Words

obtain *v* to get
something

scheme *n* a plan,
especially to do
something that is not
honest

trick *v* to make
someone believe
something that is not
true to get something
from him/her

Before You Read

1. *Do you know folktales with a clever character? Read the paragraph that
describes one type of folktale character, the trickster. Underline the key words
from the box.*

THE TRICKSTER

Folktales from around
the world have wonderful,
interesting characters. One
common folktale character
is the trickster. The
trickster shows good and
bad human qualities. In
some stories the trickster
is strong, proud,[1] and
sometimes stupid, like the
ugly, frightening trolls[2]
of Scandinavia. These
characters often have a
scheme. In the scheme,
they make weak animals do
something for them. Many
other trickster characters

are small and not strong, but they are very clever. They
carefully use their own special abilities to obtain something
they want. Examples of these tricksters are Anansi the spider
from West Africa, and the rabbit from the American South.
Tricksters often enjoy tricking other characters, but they do
not always win in the end.

---

[1] **proud** *adj* thinking that you are better or more important than other
people
[2] **troll** *n* an imaginary creature in traditional stories, like a very large
or very small ugly person

2. Work in small groups. Look at the pictures that illustrate the events in the folktale you will read. Make predictions about the tale by answering the questions. Share your ideas in small groups.

1. Who are the characters in this folktale?

2. What do you think is the problem in this story?

3. How do you predict the problem will be solved?

Global Reading

1. Read the West African folktale How Anansi Gave People Stories. *Complete the chart. Then compare your notes with a partner's.*

Time	
Place	
Characters	
Problem	
Main events of plot	
How problem is solved	

HOW ANANSI GAVE PEOPLE STORIES

1 A long, long time ago, Nyame the sky god hid all the stories in a box high in the sky. Many people and animals had tried to get the stories, but no one could do it. Because they had no stories to tell, everyone was very sad.

2 Then one day, an old spider, Anansi, made a long web all the way to the sky. Anansi climbed the web to the sky and asked Nyame, "Can I have the stories, please? I'll do anything if you give us the stories."

3 Nyame thought for a moment. Then he answered, "Fine. First I will give you a task. Bring me three things: a snake, a leopard, and bees. Then I will give you the stories." Nyame laughed so loudly that everyone on Earth could hear him!

4 Anansi climbed slowly back to Earth. How could he bring all of those things to Nyame? Anansi told his wife, Aso, what

had happened. She listened carefully. Then she said, "I have a plan." She shared her scheme with Anansi.

5 Later that day, Anansi followed Aso's plan. First, he found a long stick. After that, he went near Snake's home and said loudly, "This is very long, very long indeed!" When Snake heard Anansi talking, he said, "What is so long?" Anansi answered, "I'm sorry, Snake. You are not the longest thing anymore. This stick is longer than you are." Snake answered proudly, "It is not! I'm a very long snake! You will see that I am longer." He moved next to the stick. Then, Anansi quickly used his web to tie Snake to the stick.

6 Immediately, Anansi climbed back to the sky and gave the snake to Nyame. But Nyame only said, "I told you to bring three things. Where are the other two?" Then

(continued on next page)

Nyame laughed, "Ha ha ha!" Anansi sadly went back to Earth with no stories. He asked his wife, "How will I ever obtain the second thing, a leopard?"

7 Again, Aso had a plan, and Anansi followed it. First, he made a hole in the ground and put sticks over it so no one could see the hole. The next day, Anansi went back to the hole—and Leopard had fallen inside! Anansi used his web to quickly tie him up. He took Leopard to Nyame. Nyame looked surprised this time. He said, "You still must bring the bees!"

8 Again, Anansi asked Aso for help. Again, he followed her plan. The next day he found a tree with bees in it. He quickly threw water on the tree and on himself.

Then he said to the bees, "It is raining! Don't get wet! Quick—get inside my gourd[1]. It will keep you dry." So the bees fell for his trick and all flew into Anansi's gourd. With a big smile, Anansi used his web to close the gourd, so the bees could not get out.

9 Finally, Anansi took the bees to Nyame. Nyame was not laughing anymore. Nyame kept his promise and gave Anansi all of the stories.

10 Very carefully, Anansi carried all the stories back down to Earth. First he told the stories to his wife, Aso. Next, he told them to the other animals. Finally, he told them to the people. And after he told each story, he said, "Stories are for telling, not for keeping in boxes."

---

[1] **gourd** *n* a large fruit with a hard shell that is sometimes used as a container

2. *Work with a partner. Circle the main idea of* How Anansi Gave People Stories.

    a. Anansi gets stories from Nyame by completing difficult tasks.
    b. Anansi catches a snake, bees, and a leopard.
    c. Nyame gives Anansi a difficult task but his wife helps him complete it.

Using Time-Order Words

In a story, writers and speakers use time-order words and phrases to show when things happen. Some of the time-order words and phrases are:

First (of all) / Second / Third
Next / The next day / Later that day
Then / Just then / Immediately
After / After that / Soon after
Again
Later
Finally

Recognizing time-order words will help you follow and understand the main events of a story.

3. *Scan* How Anansi Gave People Stories. *Circle the time-order words.*

4. *Number the events to put them in the correct order.*

_____ a. Nyame gives Anansi all the stories.

_1_ b. Nyame hides all the stories in a box in the sky.

_____ c. Nyame gives Anansi three tasks.

_____ d. Anansi brings a snake, a leopard, and bees to Nyame.

_____ e. Anansi tells the stories to his wife, the other animals, and the people.

_____ f. Anansi climbs to the sky and asks for the stories.

Focused Reading

1. *Read the tale on pages 69–70 again. Then complete each question with* Who, What, When, Where, Why, *or* How. *Finally, circle the correct answers.*

1. _____ does Anansi build a web to the sky?
   a. to show his power
   b. to get the stories
   c. to tell stories

2. _____ does Nyame laugh?
   a. because he is happy to watch Anansi try to complete the tasks
   b. because he does not think Anansi can complete the tasks
   c. because he thinks Anansi is telling him a joke

3. _____ has plans for catching a snake, a leopard, and bees?
   a. Aso
   b. Anansi
   c. Nyame

4. _____ does the snake move next to?
   a. a web
   b. a stick
   c. a box

5. _____ does Anansi catch the leopard?
   a. with a web
   b. with a stick
   c. with a hole and some sticks

(continued on next page)

6. _____ do the bees go when they think it is raining?

   a. in a gourd

   b. in a web

   c. in a hole

7. _____ does Nyame stop laughing?

   a. after Anansi brings him the leopard

   b. after he gives Anansi his task

   c. after Anansi completes the task

Paraphrasing

Paraphrasing is stating someone else's ideas in your own words. While a summary gives the main points of a text in fewer words, a paraphrase usually restates a small part of a text, such as a sentence or quotation.

When you paraphrase:

- Don't change the speaker's or writer's meaning.
- Use your own words.

There are a few techniques you can use to help you paraphrase:

- Use synonyms for the key words in a sentence. Synonyms are words very close in meaning. For example, *big* and *large*.
- Change the form of the key words in a sentence (nouns to verbs, adjectives to nouns, etc.). For example, *happy—happiness*.
- Change the organization of the clauses in the sentence.

Example

Sentence: Nyame hid all of the stories in the sky so nobody could tell them.

Paraphrases:

- Nyame didn't like anyone on Earth, so he kept the stories in the sky. (not good because it changes meaning)
- Nyame kept all of the stories in the sky so no one could tell them. (not good because it does not use the person's own words; is an almost exact copy of the original sentence)
- To stop people from telling stories, Nyame kept them hidden in the sky. (good because it uses the writer's own words and doesn't change the meaning; it uses synonyms and changes the form of some key words and the organization of the clauses)

2. *Read the paraphrases of some of the sentences in the tale on pages 69–70. Find the original sentences in the tale and write them on the lines.*

   1. All the people and animals were unhappy since they couldn't tell stories.

     Because they had no stories to tell, everyone was very sad.

   2. Anansi told Nyame he would do whatever he wanted to get the stories.

     _____

3. Nyame told Anansi he had to exchange a snake, a leopard, and bees for the stories.

_____

4. Anansi told the snake that he was shorter than the stick.

_____

5. Anansi tied up the leopard with his web and took him to the sky god.

_____

3. *Read each sentence from the tale and its paraphrase. Complete the chart. Check (✓) whether the paraphrase changes the meaning, uses the same words, or is a good paraphrase. Then compare your chart with a partner's.*

	Changes Meaning	Uses the Same Words	Is a Good Paraphrase
Sentence 1: He [Anansi] asked his wife, "How will I ever get the second thing, a leopard?" **Paraphrase:** Anansi wondered how to get a leopard.			
Sentence 2: The next day, Anansi went back to the hole— and Leopard had fallen inside! **Paraphrase:** One day later, Anansi went back to the hole— and Leopard had fallen inside!			
Sentence 3: He [Anansi] quickly threw water on the tree and on himself. **Paraphrase:** Anansi threw water on the tree and on himself quickly.			
Sentence 4: With a big smile, Anansi used his web to close the gourd, so the bees could not get out. **Paraphrase:** Anansi happily closed the gourd with his web. Therefore, the bees couldn't leave.			
Sentence 5: First he [Anansi] told the stories to his wife, Aso. **Paraphrase:** Anansi loved his wife most, so he told her the stories first.			

4. *Work with a partner. Paraphrase the sentences from* How Raven Gave Light *on page 60. Make sure that you do not change the meaning and that you use your own words.*

1. [Raven] saw that the people of the world were living in the dark because an old, selfish chief was hiding the great ball of light.

_____

_____

(continued on next page)

2. Raven thought that people should not live in the dark, so he decided to bring light to them.

_____

_____

3. As soon as he had the light, the baby changed back into Raven.

_____

_____

5. *Work in small groups. Complete the Venn diagram comparing and contrasting How Raven Gave Light (page 60) and How Anansi Gave People Stories (pages 69–70). Include common characteristics of folktales. Share your diagram with the class.*

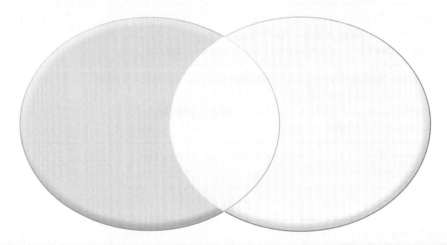

How Raven Gave Light

How Anansi Gave People Stories

Checkpoint 2   PEARSON LONGMAN myacademicconnectionslab

Before You Speak

Preparing Narrative Summaries

A **narrative summary** retells the events in a story. It quickly introduces the characters and main problem. Then it explains the plot (what happens) in correct time order. A narrative summary may conclude with a summary statement retelling the problem and its solution.

4

Building Academic Speaking Skills

In this section, you will give an oral summary of a folktale that you know. For online assignments, go to

PEARSON LONGMAN myacademicconnectionslab

1. 🎧 *Read and listen to the narrative summary of a Dutch folktale,* The Tree with the Golden Apples.

The Tree with the Golden Apples is a romantic folktale from Holland. In this story, a man gives three brothers, Jan, Dirk, and Cornelius, a task to bring him a golden apple from an island in the center of a lake. The brother who obtains an apple can marry the man's daughter, Jan's true love. At first, Jan's brothers almost reach the island by boat, but then a magic wind keeps them from the island. Next, the lake suddenly freezes, so Jan can ice-skate quickly to the tree and get a golden apple. Finally, with the help of the weather, Jan is able to complete his task and marry his true love.

2. *Work with a partner. Identify the parts of the narrative summary. Look for:*
   - the introduction of characters and the problem
   - the plot
   - the solution of the problem
   - time-order words

Focused Speaking

Giving a Narrative Summary

Follow these guidelines when preparing a written or spoken summary:
- First, make sure you understand the text well.
- Include only the major points or events necessary for understanding.
- Use your own words (paraphrase) without changing the original meaning.
- Use transition words for cohesion.

(continued on next page)

- Use time-order words to help the listeners follow the summary.
- Do not include your own ideas or opinions.

When giving a narrative summary, you can use certain expressions to help your reader.

To introduce the story, characters, and problem:

The title of the story / folktale is . . .

It is from . . .

It is about . . .

To describe the plot:

The story goes . . .

In this story, . . .

To conclude your presentation:

Finally, . . .

And that is how . . .

This story explains . . .

1. *In your notebook, write a summary of* How Anansi Gave People Stories. *Follow the guidelines for writing a summary in the skill box.*

2. *Work with a partner. Exchange your summaries. Then follow the steps.*
- Underline the title of the original story.
- Check (✓) the main events of the plot.
- Note any major points that are missing.
- Make an *X* next to any unimportant details or opinions.
- Circle the transition words.
- Note any paraphrases of statements from the text, or places where your partner should paraphrase.

3. *Give each other feedback on your summaries. Tell one thing you like, and make suggestions about things that your partner could do better. Then use your partner's suggestions to revise your summary.*

4. *Work with a new partner. Take turns giving oral summaries of* How Anansi Gave People Stories. *Use your written summary as a guide, but do not read from it directly.*

Integrated Speaking Task

You have read about the common elements of folktales, read and heard several folktales, and read and heard a model narrative summary. You will now use your knowledge of the unit content, topic vocabulary, and strategies for summarizing to give an oral narrative summary of a folktale you know.

Follow the steps to prepare for your presentation.

Step 1: Think of a folktale you know, or use the library or Internet to find one. Review the folktale and make sure you understand it well. (***Note:*** You can use the folktale you shared in Exercise 4 on page 65.)

Step 2: Complete the chart with information about your folktale.

Title and origin	
Time	
Place	
Characters	
Problem	
Main events of plot	
How problem is solved	

Step 3: Use your notes and review the skill box on page 74 and the guidelines and expressions on pages 75–76 to outline a narrative summary of your folktale. Use the summary of *The Tree with the Golden Apples* on page 75 as a model.

- In your opening sentence, introduce the common elements of folktales discussed in the lecture: the culture or tradition in which the story is based, the main characters, and the main problem in the plot.

- Following your summary, discuss at least one similarity or common element between your folktale and *How Anansi Gave People Stories*, *How Raven Gave Light*, or *The Tree with the Golden Apples*. These expressions might be useful:
  - As in *How Anansi Gave People Stories,* . . .
  - Like the character in *How Raven Gave Light,* the character in my story . . .
  - The plot/characters in both stories . . .

Step 4: Practice giving your summary.

Step 5: Work in small groups. Take turns giving your summaries. Take notes on common elements of the stories as you listen. Then discuss similarities and differences between your stories. Report your results to the class.

UNIT
5

Chemistry
Green Chemistry

Unit Description

Content: This course is designed to familiarize the student with concepts of green chemistry.

Skills: Synthesizing Information
- Recognizing relationships between different pieces of information
- Recognizing the relationship between abstract concepts and concrete information
- Recognizing the relationship between two spoken sources
- Writing a problem-solution paragraph
- Introducing problems and solutions

Unit Requirements

Readings: "Green Solutions to Challenges in Chemistry" (a scientific essay)

"Taking Green Chemistry to the Developing World" (an excerpt from a speech transcript)

Lecture: "From French Fries to Fuel"

Listening: "Driving on Vegetable Oil" (excerpts from a radio report)

Integrated Writing Task: Writing a problem-solution paragraph

Assignments: www.MyAcademicConnectionsLab.com

1

Preview

For online assignments, go to

PEARSON LONGMAN
myacademicconnectionslab

Key Words

chemistry *n* the science which studies substances like gas, metals, liquids, etc., what they are made of, and how they change; **chemical** *adj, n;* **chemist** *n*

fuel *n* a substance that provides light, heat, or power when it burns

harm *n* damage or injury; **harmful** *adj*

industry *n* the making of products in factories; **industrial** *adj*

petroleum *n* oil from beneath the ground, used for making gasoline

pollute *v* to make the air, water, or soil dirty or dangerous by adding harmful substances; **pollution** *n;* **polluted** *adj*

substance *n* a particular type of solid, liquid, or gas

Previewing the Academic Content

It is hard to imagine modern life without petroleum. Our lifestyle depends on it. We use petroleum fuel to drive cars, to heat our homes, and to fly airplanes. Petroleum is also part of hundreds of other products that we use every day, such as medicines, clothes, and toys.

However, petroleum production and its use in chemicals also causes many problems. Petroleum that gets on land and water kills many plants and animals. Burning fuels pollutes the air, and many products that are made with petroleum can be dangerous to people's health. Scientists in one modern field of chemistry, called green chemistry, are finding creative ways to make chemicals that don't cause so much harm to people and to the environment. In this unit, you will learn about green chemistry and solutions it offers to petroleum problems.

1. *How much do you know about petroleum and green chemistry? Test your knowledge. Read the statements. Decide if they are true or false. Write **T** (true) or **F** (false). Then check your answers at the bottom of the page.*

_____ 1. Petroleum may not be available to us within 40 years.

_____ 2. China uses the most petroleum in the world.

_____ 3. Saudi Arabia produces the most petroleum in the world.

_____ 4. If we use all the petroleum on land, we can get more from the oceans.

_____ 5. An important goal of green chemistry is to stop using harmful chemicals.

_____ 6. We can use safer fuels instead of petroleum.

_____ 7. Green chemistry solutions are usually very expensive.

2. *Discuss the statements and the correct answers with the class. Do any of the answers surprise you? Why or why not?*

1. T, 2. F (USA), 3. T, 4. F (we can't), 5. T, 6. T, 7. F (not very expensive)

3. Look at the cartoon. Work in small groups to answer the questions.

1. What items in the cartoon do you think use or are made with petroleum? Circle the items in the box.

bread	DVD	milk carton	shampoo
camera	glasses	pen	shoes
car	fruit	plastic bags	toothpaste
dress	lotion	purse	tree

2. Check your answers to question 1 at the bottom of the page. Think about these products and the way we use petroleum. Does anything surprise you? If so, what?

3. Describe what is happening in the cartoon. Why do you think the woman says she cares about the environment and thinks other people don't? Do you think she is right?

4. Do you use any of the items in the cartoon? If so, which ones?

5. Do you use any green products? Tell about one.

6. Which products do you think green chemists should try to make safer? Explain.

All the products in the box are made with petroleum *except* for bread, fruit, and the tree.

In this unit, you will practice synthesizing information in readings and lectures. You will also practice synthesizing information in your own writing.

Previewing the Academic Skills Focus

Synthesizing Information

In academic classes, you will often need to use different sources to find information about a topic. The sources may include written texts, lectures, discussions, graphs or charts, the Internet, or even your own knowledge about the world. Using many different sources will help you understand the topic better. When you connect information from different sources and use it to express your own ideas, you **synthesize** the information.

To synthesize information, you might connect ideas in one text to:

- other ideas in the same text (within text)
- ideas in other texts or lectures (text to text)
- your experience or personal knowledge (text to self)
- commonly known facts or events (text to world)

1. Look at the graph and read the excerpt from an article.

Average World Temperatures and Fossil Fuel[1] Use

In the past 50 years, Earth's temperatures have been increasing quickly. Richard Wool of the University of Delaware writes, "We have a very, very serious problem . . . called global warming." (2007) Global warming, the increase in Earth's temperatures, may have serious effects on our planet, including dangerous weather and storms. Many experts agree that pollution from burning fossil fuels like petroleum can cause global warming. John Warner of the University of Massachusetts in Lowell, says people who make chemicals need to think about the consequences. They should take steps to make products cleaner and safer to use.

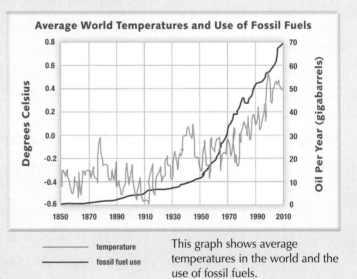

This graph shows average temperatures in the world and the use of fossil fuels.

---

[1] **fossil fuels** *n* fuels, such as gas and oil, that formed from plants and animals that lived millions of years ago

2. *Complete the tasks.*

1. What information did you learn from the graph and the excerpt? Complete the chart. Note any new information in the *Information from Graph* and *Information from Excerpt* boxes. Then compare your answers with a partner's.

Information from Graph	Information from Excerpt
The use of fossil fuels . . .	Burning fossil fuels . . .
Information from Self—My Experience	**Information from World—Common Knowledge**
I use petroleum for . . .	More people have cars and are using more petroleum.

2. What experience or common knowledge do you have about petroleum and global warming? Write it in the *Information from Self* and *Information from World* boxes. Share your information with the class.

3. *How does synthesizing information from different sources help you understand a topic? Discuss it with the class.*

2

Building Academic Reading Skills

In this section, you will practice recognizing the relationship between abstract concepts and concrete information. For online assignments, go to

Before You Read

1. *Green chemistry is based on a group of principles, or rules, that green chemists use in their work. Match the principles on the left with the paraphrases on the right.*

Principles of Green Chemistry

_____ 1. No chemical waste.

_____ 2. Make chemicals that break down naturally.

_____ 3. Use renewable resources and not nonrenewable resources.

_____ 4. Make safer chemicals.

Paraphrases

a. Any chemicals we make should not be toxic.

b. Only use materials that we can make or get more of.

c. Chemical processes should not make materials that people don't want or can't clean up.

d. Only make chemicals that naturally change into something that is not harmful.

2. *Read the advertisement from a company that sells green products. Which principle (or principles) of green chemistry listed in Exercise 1 does each product follow? Write* **1**, **2**, **3**, *or* **4**.

GREEN WORLD COMPANY

| HOUSEHOLD | BOOKS | SALE |

"Green" Bowls

These bowls are made from 100 percent renewable sugarcane plants. They change into smaller and smaller pieces that do not harm the environment. In fact, they turn into dirt that can be used to grow plants.

Principles: _____

Paint

This paint benefits you, your family, and our Earth. It contains no harmful chemicals that pollute the air inside your home. Also, the color in this paint comes from natural materials.

Principles: _____

Laundry Detergent

Wash your clothes the green way! The scientists who made this laundry soap used only natural ingredients, not dangerous toxins. The bottle is biodegradable, too.

Principles: _____

3. *Work in small groups. Discuss the questions.*

1. Do you use any green products? If not, why? If so, which green products do you use?

2. Do you know of other similar companies or green products? Do you think a green company can make a big difference to us and the environment? Explain.

Global Reading

1. *Read the essay written by a green chemist. Then write the number of the paragraph next to its main idea.*

_____ Green chemists must think about the effects of their alternative fuels.

_____ Biofuels are less dangerous than fossil fuels.

_____ People want and need chemical products that are safe.

_____ One opportunity that green chemistry offers is finding alternatives to fossil fuels.

_____ Biofuels have negative consequences, too.

GREEN SOLUTIONS TO CHALLENGES IN CHEMISTRY

1 Modern chemistry is a field in trouble. According to a recent study,[1] 60 percent of Europeans have negative views of the chemical industry. Another study[2] showed that 74 percent of Americans have similar feelings. These results show that people are worried about the harmful effects that chemicals have on people and the environment. Over the last 80 years, chemists have made much of modern life possible, but today we need products that help people without causing harm to the environment or costing too much.

2 In 1998, green chemistry began. Its main goals are to stop new environmental problems and to provide solutions to the problems we already have. In this way, green chemistry offers new opportunities to the field of chemistry. One important goal of green chemistry today is finding ways to stop the world's dependence on petroleum. Since petroleum is expensive, toxic, and likely to be gone within 40 years, it is even more important to find safe and clean solutions.

3 In recent years, green chemists have made biofuels from plants and other natural materials. This solution follows several important principles of green chemistry. First, biofuels come from renewable materials such as soybeans and corn, which grow quickly. Second, making biofuel produces 60 to 80 percent less toxic waste than producing petroleum fuels. Also, burning biofuels causes much less pollution than burning petroleum fuel. Finally, biofuels naturally change into materials that do not harm the environment. So if biofuels get on land or in water, they are easier and less expensive to clean up. For all these reasons, biofuels seem like a good solution.

4 Biofuels are not a perfect solution to petroleum fuels, however. Scientists

---

[1] Pan European Image Survey, European Chemical Industry Council (CEFIC), 1994.
[2] Corporate Image of the Chemical Industry, CIA (UK), 1993.

(continued on next page)

have found that biofuels also have negative consequences. For example, today biofuel production is the biggest cause of rain forest destruction in the Amazon, because trees are cut to grow plants for fuel. Biofuel production has also resulted in higher food prices in many countries because companies and farmers make more money growing plants for biofuel than growing them for food. Finally, producing biofuels causes pollution. Farmers use pesticides to grow corn for ethanol, a chemical used to make biofuel. This causes a lot of pollution. In addition, making ethanol puts dangerous toxins in the air.

5 Finding a solution to our dependence on petroleum fuel is an important goal for green chemists. However, scientists must carefully study the effects of every possible solution. In this way, green chemistry can be "the solution, not the problem."

Recognizing Relationships between Different Pieces of Information

To synthesize different pieces of information, you need to be able to notice the connections between them. When comparing information, you might notice ideas that are:

- similar
- different
- specific examples of general ideas
- solutions
- reasons
- causes and effects

2. Work with a partner. Identify the relationships between the pieces of information from the reading. Circle the correct answer to complete each statement.

1. The writer presents the negative views people have of the chemical industry as a(n) _____ the field of chemistry is in trouble.
   a. reason why   b. example of why

2. The beginning of green chemistry was a(n) _____ our need for safe products.
   a. effect of   b. reason for

3. Biofuels are a(n) _____ the problem of petroleum fuel.
   a. reason for   b. solution to

4. Problems with biofuels are _____ those with petroleum fuel.
   a. similar to   b. different from

3. Complete the solutions with the correct words from the box. Then match the problems on the left with the solutions on the right.

green chemistry   green products   scientists

Problems

_____ 1. Chemical products are dangerous to our health.

_____ 2. Humans depend too much on petroleum, a harmful nonrenewable chemical.

_____ 3. Use of biofuels has caused destruction of rain forests, high food prices, and pollution.

Solutions

a. _____ stops new problems and offers solutions to existing ones.

b. There is no perfect solution, but _____ are looking.

c. _____ are safe and renewable.

Focused Reading

1. Read the essay on pages 85–86 again and complete the chart. Check (✓) the correct columns.

	Reason for Making Biofuels	Effect of Making Biofuels
Petroleum is toxic.		
People want clean and safe products.		
There is destruction of rain forest in the Amazon.		
There is less food.		
People worry about dangerous chemicals.		
Ethanol is putting toxins in the air.		
Fossil fuels pollute the air when burned.		

Abstract concepts are based on general ideas or principles. They are usually not very specific.

Example

Biofuel is becoming more popular.

Concrete information is specific. Concrete information is often used to make an abstract concept clear. Concrete information includes facts, details, and examples.

Example

Biofuel production in the United States grew 200 percent from 2004 to 2005.

In academic texts, main ideas are often abstract concepts. The supporting facts, details, and examples provide concrete information.

2. *Write the abstract statements from the box that match their concrete information. Compare your answers with a partner's.*

Abstract statements about biofuels

The production of biofuels follows several important green chemistry principles.

~~Biofuels are safer than fossil fuels.~~

Biofuels use renewable resources.

Producing biofuels has some negative effects.

---

1. **Abstract statement:** *Biofuels are safer than fossil fuels.*

   Concrete statements about biofuels:
   - If biofuels get on land or in water, they are easier and less expensive to clean up.
   - When produced and burned, biofuels cause less pollution than petroleum.

2. **Abstract statement:** _____

   Concrete statements about biofuels:
   - Plants used for biofuels grow back quickly.
   - Biofuels are made from soybeans and corn.

3. **Abstract statement:** _____

   Concrete statements about biofuels:
   - When produced and burned, biofuels cause less pollution than petroleum.
   - Biofuels break down into harmless substances.

4. **Abstract statement:** _____

   Concrete etatements about biofuels:
   - People are cutting trees in rain forests to grow plants for biofuels.
   - Pesticides for growing corn are causing pollution.

3. *Discuss the questions in small groups.*

   1. What are the advantages and disadvantages of using petroleum?

   2. What are the advantages and disadvantages of using biofuels?

| Checkpoint 1 | PEARSON LONGMAN myacademicconnectionslab |

Before You Listen

1. *You will listen to a lecture by Dr. Steven Schultz, a green chemist. Before you listen, study Dr. Schultz's class handout.*

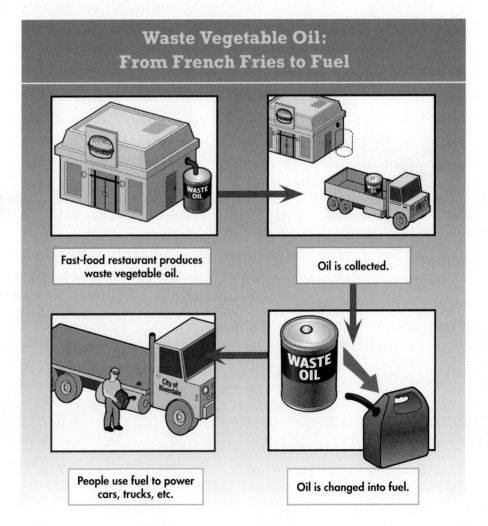

Waste Vegetable Oil: From French Fries to Fuel

Fast-food restaurant produces waste vegetable oil.

Oil is collected.

People use fuel to power cars, trucks, etc.

Oil is changed into fuel.

2. Work with a partner. Make predictions about the lecture based on Dr. Schultz's handout on page 89. Answer the questions.

1. What do you think the lecture will be about?

2. What is waste vegetable oil?

3. What are the possible advantages and disadvantages of using vegetable oil?

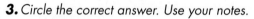

Global Listening

1. 🎧 Listen to an excerpt from the lecture. Take notes in your notebook on the three main ideas Dr. Schultz will talk about. Then compare your notes with a partner's.

2. 🎧 Listen to the whole lecture. Check (✓) the statement that is the best paraphrase of the main idea of the entire lecture. Discuss your answers with the class.

_____ Scientists are excited because they have found a good solution to today's fuel problems.

_____ Waste vegetable oil has two roles. First, it cooks food. Then it fuels cars and trucks.

_____ Waste vegetable oil is a good solution to petroleum fuel because it is already available, doesn't cost much, and is simple to use.

3. Circle the correct answer. Use your notes.

1. According to the lecture, what is waste vegetable oil (WVO)?
   a. oil that we cannot use again
   b. oil that we have already used once
   c. oil that we use to make food

2. According to Dr. Schultz, what is the biggest advantage of WVO?
   a. It is cheaper than petroleum-based fuel.
   b. Restaurants give it away for free.
   c. It changes waste into a valuable product.

3. What does the lecture NOT say about WVO?
   a. It has many advantages for people and the environment.
   b. It is better for cars than petroleum-based fuel.
   c. It is cheaper than petroleum-based fuel.

4. Which cars can run on WVO?
   a. any cars that run on regular diesel fuel
   b. only cars with a special part
   c. cars that were built to run on WVO

Focused Listening

1. 🎧 *Read the sentences. Each sentence has information that is wrong. Listen to the lecture again. Then rewrite the sentences with the correct information. Compare your corrected sentences with a partner's.*

1. WVO means "waste valuable oil."
   WVO means "waste vegetable oil."
   _____

2. WVO comes from cooking oil used in homes.
   _____

3. The United States produced over 11 million liters of WVO in 2000.
   _____

4. A lot of new plants have to grow to make WVO.
   _____

5. Dr. Schultz works with families who want to use WVO.
   _____

6. Some cars need a special driver to use WVO.
   _____

2. *Listen to the excerpts from the lecture. Write short answers.*

🎧 **Excerpt One**

What does Dr. Schultz suggest that people might think about chemists?
_____

🎧 **Excerpt Two**

What does Dr. Schultz suggest about the American diet?
_____

Recognizing the Relationship between Two Spoken Sources

In academic classes, you will need to connect ideas from many sources you hear (spoken sources) for a better understanding of a topic. These spoken sources include lectures, conversations, classroom or group discussions, television, radio, and the Internet.

To connect ideas from two spoken sources, take notes on each source and compare them. Make sure you understand the ideas in each source.

3. 🎧 *Listen to excerpts from a radio report on using waste vegetable oil to power cars. In the* Excerpt *column of the chart, take notes on what each person says. Then compare your notes with a partner's. You will use the other columns of the chart later.*

Excerpt	Ideas from the Lecture	Relationship between Ideas (Agree/Disagree)
1. Kent Glass, reporter *WVO=good alternative* *Oil=used twice* *Driving car = better for environment*	Using waste vegetable oil is like turning garbage into gold.	
2. Peter Berger, WVO user	WVO is cheap.	
3. Peter Berger, WVO user	WVO is easy to use.	
4. Kim Wei, environmental studies expert	WVO is a simple and green alternative to petroleum fuel.	

4. *Compare the notes you took on each excerpt with the information in the* Ideas from the Lecture *column. In the* Relationship between Ideas *column, write* ***Agree*** *or* ***Disagree*** *to describe how the speaker in the excerpt would probably feel about the idea from the lecture.*

5. *Discuss the questions in small groups.*

1. Which green chemistry principles from page 83 does WVO follow?

2. How does WVO compare to other fuels you have learned about? Explain your answers.

In my opinion, WVO is better than other biofuels because . . .

3. What are some other solutions to our dependence on petroleum? What can we do as individuals and in our communities?

Checkpoint 2   PEARSON LONGMAN myacademicconnectionslab

Before You Write

Writing a Problem-Solution Paragraph

A problem-solution paragraph describes a problem. Then it explains a solution or possible solutions to the problem. A problem-solution paragraph typically includes three parts:

- a topic sentence with a description of the problem
- a body with a description of (a) possible solution(s)
- a conclusion with an explanation of how the solution is helpful

Read a transcript from a talk given by Martyn Poliakoff, a chemist at the University of Nottingham. Then answer the questions on page 94.

Taking Green Chemistry to the Developing World

Recently I was asked to introduce the ideas of green chemistry to a group of high school students and teachers at Wachamo Comprehensive High School in Hossana, Ethiopia. The problem was that I wasn't sure of the best way to explain green chemistry simply. My solution was to use an example of a plastic bag that I got two days earlier at the town's market. They make bags like these from petroleum from other countries because Ethiopia does not have much petroleum of its own. After people use these bags, they throw them away. On the road I counted 12 bags that people had thrown away in just 100 meters on my way to the school. By contrast, Ethiopia produces a lot of sugarcane. If people there made the bags from sugarcane, then Ethiopia would not have to buy its bags—or oil to make bags—from other countries. More

(continued on next page)

4

Building Academic Writing Skills

In this section, you will practice writing problem-solution paragraphs. Then you will write a paragraph about a modern problem related to green chemistry. You will synthesize information and use vocabulary from the readings and the lecture.
For online assignments, go to

PEARSON LONGMAN myacademicconnectionslab

importantly, cows would be able to eat the used bags in the street! This simple example helped me explain the goals of green chemistry to everyone. Making bags from sugarcane needs new chemistry—it needs green chemistry.[1]

Children collecting plastic bags in Hossana

[1] Together with Proctor and Gamble and Ethiopian chemists, Poliakoff is developing plastic bags made from local sugarcane.

Poliakoff, M., & Noda, I. (2004.) Plastic bags, sugar cane and advanced vibrational spectroscopy: taking green chemistry to the Third World. *Green Chemistry, 6.*

1. What problem does the topic sentence introduce?

2. What is the proposed solution? According to the paragraph, why is it a good solution? Give details.

3. What is the conclusion? How is it connected to the topic sentence?

4. What is your opinion about Poliakoff's solution? Do you think it is a good one? Why or why not?

Focused Writing

Introducing Problems and Solutions

When writing a problem-solution paragraph, you can use certain expressions to make your points clear.

To introduce a problem:

The problem is/was _____.

_____ is one of the main problems.

One difficulty is _____.

To introduce a solution:

His/Her/Their/My solution is/was _____.

One way to solve this problem is _____.

_____ is a great way to solve the problem of _____.

1. *Read the transcript from Martyn Poliakoff's talk on pages 93–94 again. Underline the expressions he uses to introduce the problem and solution.*

2. *In his talk, Poliakoff describes the plastic bag problem in Ethiopia. Follow the instructions to write a short paragraph about the problem.*

1. Complete the chart using the information from Poliakoff's presentation.

Plastic Bag Problem	Solution to Plastic Bag Problem

2. Write your paragraph. Be sure to include:
   - the problem
   - the proposed solution(s)
   - a conclusion
   - expressions to introduce problems and solutions

3. Work with a partner. Exchange paragraphs. Use the questions to comment on each other's paragraph.
   - Does the topic sentence introduce the problem?
   - Does the body explain the proposed solution?
   - Does the conclusion explain how the solution is helpful?
   - Did your partner use expressions to introduce problems and solutions?

Integrated Writing Task

You have listened to a lecture and read texts about green chemistry and the modern problem of plastic bags. You will now use your knowledge of the unit content, topic vocabulary, synthesizing information, and writing a problem-solution paragraph to write a paragraph answering this question: **What is the best solution to solve the worldwide plastic bag problem?**

Follow the steps to write your paragraph.

Step 1: Read more about the global plastic bag problem. Check (✓) the facts that are most important to you.

Fast Facts about Plastic Bags

○ Each year, people around the world use about 500 billion to 1 trillion plastic bags.

○ Plastic bags are made from petroleum, and the used bags cause a lot of pollution.

○ Each year, people throw away 4 billion plastic bags.

○ Animals that eat plastic bags can die from the toxins.

○ Plastic bags pollute the dirt and water in the ground as they break down into smaller and smaller pieces.

○ It takes plastic 450 years to break down in water.

○ It takes plastic 1,000 years to break down on land.

Step 2: Many countries are trying to solve the plastic bag problem. Read the possible solutions. Consider the pros (positive reasons) and cons (negative reasons). Choose the solution that you think is best. You may also choose your own solution based on the principles of green chemistry. (Note: Your solution must be different from Poliakoff's solution on pages 93–94.)

SOLUTION 1: Change waste plastic back into oil.

PRO: Plastics don't have to be clean. Waste plastic goes through a process under heat and is then turned into valuable diesel fuel.

CON: Only certain plastics can be used. If the wrong plastic is mixed in, the diesel fuel cannot be sold. The process of changing plastic into oil causes pollution and puts many toxins in the air.

SOLUTION 2: Use plastic made of plants.

PRO: These bags break down more quickly than bags made from petroleum, and they are made from renewable resources.

CON: The process of growing plants to make this plastic uses pesticides, land, and freshwater, and this harms the environment.

SOLUTION 3: Recycle used bags to make new ones.

PRO: It keeps bags out of landfills.[1]

CON: Only certain plastic bags can be reused, and it is hard to separate them. It is more expensive to recycle plastic bags than to make new plastic bags.

SOLUTION 4: (choose your own)

PRO:

CON:

---

[1] **landfill** *n* a place where waste is buried in large amounts

Step 3: Work with a partner. Look for connections among the plastic bag issue, the green chemistry principles, and the concepts and ideas in this unit. Discuss the questions and take notes.

- How is the plastic bag problem similar to problems related to petroleum fuel and biofuel use?
- Are there any similarities between the solution you chose and the solutions of biofuel and WVO offered for the petroleum problem? Does the solution you chose have possible negative consequences?
- Which green chemistry principles relate to your proposed solution?

Step 4: Complete the chart with ideas you want to write about in your paragraph. To support your ideas, make connections to ideas from the listenings and readings in this unit.

Topic sentence (describe the problem)	
Body (describe the solution or possible solutions)	
Conclusion (explain how the solution is or would be helpful)	

Step 5: Use your notes from Step 4 to write a problem-solution paragraph about plastic bags. Use the vocabulary and skills you learned in this unit, including expressions that introduce problems and solutions.

Step 6: Exchange paragraphs with a partner. Use the checklist for feedback.

Feedback Checklist	Yes	No
Does the topic sentence introduce the problem?		
Does the body explain the proposed solution?		
Does the conclusion explain how the solution is/could be helpful?		
Did your partner use expressions to introduce the problem?		
Did your partner use expressions to introduce the solution?		

Step 7: Rewrite your paragraph based on your partner's feedback.

Step 8: Discuss your proposed solutions as a class. Do you agree with other classmates' solutions? Which solution do you think is best? Why?

Art History
The Art of Marc Chagall

Unit Description

Content: This course is designed to familiarize the student with the life and art of Marc Chagall.

Skills: Fact and Opinion

- Identifying facts
- Identifying opinions
- Recognizing a speaker's degree of certainty
- Identifying support for opinions
- Giving and supporting an opinion
- Showing agreement and disagreement

Unit Requirements

Reading: "Themes in Chagall's Art" (an excerpt from an art history textbook)

Lecture: "Chagall: Style and Criticism"

Listening: A discussion of Lyubov Popova's *Lady with the Guitar*

Integrated Speaking Task: Participating in a group discussion about a painting by Marc Chagall

Assignments: www.MyAcademicConnectionsLab.com

Marc Chagall. *The Birthday*. 1915. Oil on canvas.

Previewing the Academic Content

The late nineteenth and early twentieth centuries were a time of great change in art. Before this time, artists tried to make paintings look realistic. The new artists, like Pablo Picasso, used an abstract style to show ideas about people and objects without showing how they looked in reality. They shocked the art world with their modern techniques. In one such kind of art—cubism—images were made up of shapes like circles and squares or patterns seen from different views. These objects and people did not look real. Russian artist Marc Chagall was greatly influenced by the abstract work and artists of his time, but Chagall is famous for his own style of modern art. In this unit, you will explore the life and work of Marc Chagall.

1. *Many artists paint self-portraits, or pictures of themselves. Study the three self-portraits. They are examples of three different styles of art. Number the paintings from 1 (most realistic) to 3 (most abstract). Then work in small groups to answer the questions.*

Vincent Van Gogh.
Self-Portrait with Pipe and Straw Hat. 1888. Oil on canvas.

———————

Marc Chagall.
Self-Portrait with Seven Fingers. 1913. Oil on canvas.

———————

Peter Paul Rubens.
Self-Portrait. 1638–1640. Oil on canvas.

———————

1. What makes the paintings realistic? What makes them abstract?

2. Which paintings do you like? Which ones do you not like? Why?

2. *Like Chagall, many artists in the early twentieth century were influenced by the new abstract style in art. Lyubov Popova was one such artist. Work with a partner. Compare Popova's painting* Lady with the Guitar *to Chagall's* I and the Village *on the next page. Then discuss the questions with a partner. Use the key words in your discussion.*

abstract *adj* art made of shapes and patterns that do not look like real people or things

cubism *n* a 20th-century style of art in which objects and people are shown with geometric shapes; **cubist** *adj*

image *n* a picture

pattern *n* an arrangement of shapes, lines, and colors

reality *n* things that actually happen or are true; **realistic** *adj*

style *n* a way of doing or creating something

subject *n* the thing or person in a painting or photograph

Lyubov Popova.
Lady with the Guitar. 1913–1914.
Oil on canvas.

Marc Chagall.
I and the Village. 1911.
Oil on canvas.

1. What similarities and differences do you see between Chagall's and Popova's paintings? Consider the colors, shapes, and subjects of the paintings.

2. Why do you think the artists made these paintings? Was it to tell a story, to create an emotion, to show an event, or to do something else? Explain.

3. Do you like the paintings? Why or why not?

3. *What do you think these quotations about art mean? Circle the best answer.*

Quotation 1: *Why do you try to understand art? Do you try to understand the song of a bird?* —Pablo Picasso
   a. Picasso thinks people should try to understand art.
   b. Picasso thinks people should not try to understand art.

Quotation 2: *Unlike abstract painters, it is important for [Chagall] that people who see his paintings understand what he is trying to show."* —Jean-Michel Foray, director of the Chagall Museum in France[1]
   a. Chagall thinks his art should be easy to understand.
   b. Chagall thinks his art does not have to be easy to understand.

---

[1] Adapted from Michels, S. (2003, August 19). Celebrating Chagall. *Online NewsHour.* Retrieved on May 22, 2009 from http://www.pbs.org.

(continued on next page)

Quotation 3: *[Marc Chagall] is a painter, of course, and what a painter. But above all a storyteller. Chagall tells us his life, tells us about himself. He tells us of events.* —Francois Le Target, author of *Marc Chagall* [2]

    a. Chagall's paintings tell a story.

    b. Chagall was a better storyteller than painter.

4. *Discuss the questions in small groups.*
- Do you think people should be able to understand art? Explain.
- Do you think art that tells a story is more interesting than other types of art? Explain.

In this unit, you will learn how to distinguish (tell the difference between) fact and opinion, to recognize a speaker or writer's degree of certainty, and to express and support an opinion.

Previewing the Academic Skills Focus

Fact and Opinion

Facts are true statements that we can test or prove, such as numbers or dates. An **opinion** is someone's thought, belief, or feeling about something. Recognizing the difference between facts and opinions is important for evaluating—judging the value of—what you read and hear. In college courses, students are often asked to express their opinions and to support them with facts and good reasons.

Read the statements about Marc Chagall. Write **Facts** *above the column with statements that can be proven to be true. Write* **Opinions** *above the column with statements that express feelings or beliefs. Discuss your answers as a class.*

• Marc Chagall was born in 1887. • Chagall was Russian. • He used bright colors in his art. • He used cubist ideas in his early paintings. • Chagall lived and worked in Paris for many years. • Chagall's wife's name was Bella.	• Marc Chagall's art is too joyful. • Chagall is the best artist of the twentieth century. • Chagall's paintings tell interesting stories from his life. • Chagall was probably a happy person. • Chagall's paintings look like pictures from a dream.

---

[2] Le Target, F. (1985). *Marc Chagall*. New York: Rizzoli International Publications.

2

Building Academic Reading Skills

In this section, you will practice distinguishing between facts and opinions.
For online assignments, go to

myacademicconnectionslab

Key Words

dreamlike *adj* as if happening in a dream

fantasy *n* an experience or situation that you imagine but is not real; **fantastic** *adj*

independent *adj* not controlled by other people

inspire *v* to make someone want to do something

modernism *n* a style of art and building that was especially popular from the 1940s to the 1960s, in which artists used simple shapes; **modernistic** *adj*

theme *n* the main idea or subject in a book, movie, painting, speech, etc.

universal *adj* true or right in every situation

Before You Read

1. *Read the timeline of Marc Chagall's life.*

WORLD EVENTS		MARC CHAGALL'S LIFE	
		1887	Chagall is born into a large Jewish family in Vitebsk, Russia.
Pablo Picasso and Georges Braque begin to develop the cubist style of art.	1906–1908	1907–1910	Chagall studies many styles of art in St. Petersburg, Russia. He is in jail for a short time because he does not have a permit[1] to live there. At this time, Jews need a permit to live in St. Petersburg.
		1910–1914	Chagall lives in Paris, France. Cubist and modernist artists inspire him, but he develops his own independent style. Chagall paints some of his most famous work, showing many universal themes.
World War I begins.	1914	1914	Chagall returns to Russia.
		1915	Chagall marries Bella Rosenfeld, who is the subject of many of his paintings.
		1916	Chagall's daughter Ida is born.
The Russian Revolution happens.	1917		
World War I ends.	1918		
		1923	Chagall returns to Paris with his wife and daughter.
World War II begins.	1939		Chagall lives in Paris. Nazis destroy much of his art.
The Nazis occupy[2] Europe and persecute[3] Jews.		1941	Chagall lives in the United States.
		1944	Bella dies.
World War II ends.	1945		
		1948	Chagall moves from the United States back to Paris, France.
		1952	Chagall marries Valentina Brodsky.
		1958	Chagall begins working on larger projects, such as colorful glass windows in public and religious buildings.
		1985	Chagall dies in Saint-Paul de Vence, France.

[1] **permit** *n* an official written statement giving a person the right to do something
[2] **occupy** *v* to enter a place in a large group and keep control of it, especially by military force
[3] **persecute** *v* to treat someone badly because of his or her religious or political beliefs

2. *Discuss the questions in small groups. Use the facts from the timeline on page 103.*

1. In which countries did Chagall live? Where did he spend the most time?

2. What did Chagall study in St. Petersburg?

3. Who was an important subject in Chagall's art?

4. When did Chagall move to the United States?

5. Where did Chagall die?

3. *Use the information in the timeline to form opinions about Chagall's life. Discuss your opinions in small groups.*

1. When do you think Chagall was happiest? Why?

2. When do you think Chagall was saddest? Why?

3. How do you think Chagall felt about Bella? Why?

4. Why do you think Chagall lived in the United States during World War II?

5. Starting in 1944, Chagall stopped painting for some time. What do you think was the reason?

Global Reading

1. *Read the excerpt from an art history textbook. As you read, underline the opinions. Take notes on the main ideas.*

Themes in Chagall's Art

Home, nature, and love are some of the main subjects in artist Marc Chagall's work. These subjects show what was most important to Chagall. In addition, they are universal themes that made Chagall a popular artist whose work many people understand and enjoy. According to Marc Scheps (1987) in *Marc Chagall: 100th Anniversary of His Birth*, "Chagall more than any other artist in the twentieth century" was able to turn "the personal into the universal."

One of Chagall's early and best-known paintings, *I and the Village* (1911), clearly shows the themes of nature and home. The soft, dreamlike images in the painting show simple times and traditions. The place in the painting must be Vitebsk, the small Russian farming village where Chagall was born into a large Jewish family. Chagall's paintings often show images of his village. The painting brings together bright colors and Jewish and Russian elements to show the relationships between people and nature, life and death. The main part of the painting shows a green man (probably Chagall himself) and an animal (a horse or a goat) looking at each other. A circle connects the

Marc Chagall.
I and the Village.
1911.
Oil on canvas.

two images. This could be an example of Chagall's belief in a strong connection between humans and animals. The painting also shows life, through the plant in the man's hands, and death, in the image of a farmer holding a cutter. In *I and the Village,* Chagall brings together fantasy and reality to show a love of home and the natural world.

Love is another key theme in Chagall's paintings, especially those of his first wife, Bella. Chagall married Bella in 1915. Her role in Chagall's life and art was very important. Chagall painted many images of them together, and these works clearly show the feelings of romantic love and joy he felt for her. Even after her death in 1944, Bella continued to inspire his work.

Chagall continued using these themes as he developed his independent artistic style. He learned about cubism while living in Paris, where many famous modernist artists of the time lived. Chagall said, "I owe all I have done to Paris," yet he never was part of any art movement.[1] Chagall's power is in the way he used the cubist and abstract styles of his time to create his own dreamlike images of the subjects he loved.

---

[1] **movement** *n* a group of people who share the same ideas or beliefs and who work together to complete a particular goal

Chagall, M. (1987). *Marc Chagall: 100th anniversary of his birth: The Marcus Dienner Collection.* Tel Aviv: Tel Aviv Museum.

2. *Read the statements. Decide if they are true or false. Write **T** (true) or **F** (false). Then check your answers with the class. Discuss any differences in your answers.*

_____ 1. Chagall's themes include love, nature, and home.

_____ 2. Chagall painted subjects that were important in his own life.

_____ 3. He showed themes that weren't interesting to many people.

_____ 4. The main theme of *I and the Village* is love.

_____ 5. *I and the Village* shows a connection between humans and animals.

_____ 6. Chagall's paintings are completely realistic.

_____ 7. Paris was an important place to Chagall.

Identifying Facts

A fact is information that is true for everyone. In other words, it can be tested or proven. For example:

Marc Chagall was a Russian artist.

I and the Village is a painting.

To find facts, ask yourself, "Can this be proven to be true?" If the answer is *yes,* then it is a fact. Recognizing and remembering important facts can help you understand any subject. Including facts in your own writing and speech will help you support your own ideas.

3. Study the painting I and the Village on page 104. Write four facts about the painting. Then read your facts to a partner. Your partner will listen and decide if your statements are facts. If a statement is not a fact, correct it or write a new one. Then switch roles.

Example

A: In *I and the Village* there is a big green face.
B: Yes, that's a fact.
A: The green face looks very strange.
B: No, that's not a fact. You can't prove it.

Focused Reading

1. Read the text on pages 105–105 again. Circle the best answer to complete each statement.

1. According to Marc Scheps, Chagall's paintings show themes that are _____.
   a. not personal   b. universal   c. dreamlike

2. *I and the Village* shows a _____ village.
   a. French   b. Russian   c. Jewish

3. *I and the Village* brings together Russian and _____ elements.
   a. modern   b. French   c. Jewish

4. Chagall had a deep love for _____.
   a. the universe   b. cubism   c. the natural world

5. Chagall developed his independent style in _____.
   a. Paris   b. New York   c. Vitebsk

Identifying Opinions

Recognizing opinions is an important part of evaluating a text. An **opinion** is a person's thought, belief, or feeling about something. An opinion is often introduced by specific phrases, such as:

I think (that) . . ., I believe (that) . . ., I feel (that) . . ., In my opinion . . .

Words such as *good, bad, best, beautiful,* are also used in opinions.

Example

I think that Marc Chagall's art is *beautiful.*

Sometimes an opinion does not use expressions like these. In that case, to decide if a statement is an opinion, ask yourself these questions:

Can I check or prove this?   If you answer *no,* it is an opinion.
Can I agree or disagree?   If you answer *yes,* it is an opinion.

Example

The colors in Chagall's paintings are too bright. (This is an opinion because you can agree or disagree with it.)

2. *Read the excerpts from the reading. Each excerpt contains an opinion, a fact, or both. Underline facts once. Underline opinions twice. Then compare your answers with a partner's. Are there any expressions that helped you decide which statements are opinions? If so, what are they?*

Example

The main part of the painting shows a green man (probably Chagall himself) and an animal (a horse or a goat) looking at each other.

1. The place in the painting must be Vitebsk, the small Russian farming village where Chagall was born into a large Jewish family.

2. A circle connects the two images. This could be an example of Chagall's belief in a strong connection between humans and animals.

3. In *I and the Village*, Chagall brings together fantasy and reality to show a love of home and the natural world.

4. Chagall married Bella in 1915.

5. Chagall painted many images of them together, and these works clearly show the feelings of romantic love and joy he felt for her.

6. Even after her death in 1944, Bella continued to inspire his work.

3. *For homework, an art professor has asked students to share thoughts on the class blog about Chagall's painting* I and the Village. *Their responses should include at least one fact about the painting and two or more personal opinions. Read two students' entries. Underline the facts once. Underline the opinions twice. Did both writers include a fact and two or more opinions? Compare your answers with a partner's.*

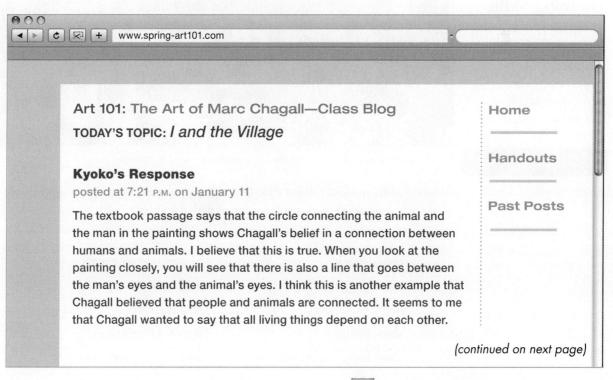

Art 101: The Art of Marc Chagall—Class Blog

TODAY'S TOPIC: *I and the Village*

Home

Handouts

Past Posts

Kyoko's Response
posted at 7:21 P.M. on January 11

The textbook passage says that the circle connecting the animal and the man in the painting shows Chagall's belief in a connection between humans and animals. I believe that this is true. When you look at the painting closely, you will see that there is also a line that goes between the man's eyes and the animal's eyes. I think this is another example that Chagall believed that people and animals are connected. It seems to me that Chagall wanted to say that all living things depend on each other.

(continued on next page)

Tatiana's Response

posted at 11:43 p.m. on January 11

The title of the painting is *I and the Village*. I think the "I" from the title
is the green man in the painting. The textbook says that the man is
probably Chagall himself. He's wearing a schoolboy hat, so I think it's
Chagall when he was a boy. In my opinion, Chagall is showing that he will
always remember the place where he grew up.

4. *Write your own blog entry on a separate piece of paper. Make sure to include
at least one fact and at least two opinions. Then exchange entries with a
partner. Underline the facts once and the opinions twice.*

Checkpoint 1　　PEARSON LONGMAN myacademicconnectionslab

Before You Listen

3

**Building
Academic
Listening Skills**

In this section, you will
practice recognizing
a speaker's degree
of certainty when
expressing opinions.
For online assignments,
go to

PEARSON LONGMAN
myacademicconnectionslab

People create and enjoy art for many reasons. It has many purposes.

1. *What is the purpose of art? Check (✓) the opinions that you agree with. Then
discuss your opinions in small groups or with the class.*

Art should . . .

_____ create beauty　　　　　　_____ show important events

_____ tell a story　　　　　　　_____ inspire people to change

_____ help people relax　　　　_____ show reality

_____ show nature　　　　　　　_____ be easy to understand

_____ show universal themes　　_____ inspire strong emotions

2. Read the quotations by famous artists. Which opinion(s) from Exercise 1 does each quotation support? Write it in the chart. Then compare your chart with a partner's.

Artist	Statement	Opinion it Supports
Henri Matisse	"Art should be something like a good armchair in which to rest."	*help people relax*
Claude Monet	"I can only draw what I see."	
Norman Rockwell	"My . . . purpose is to [explain] the typical American. I guess I am a storyteller."	
Marc Chagall	"Only love interests me, and I am only in contact with things I love."	
Pablo Picasso	"What I want is that my picture should [inspire] nothing but emotion."	
Vincent van Gogh	"In painting I want to say something comforting in the way that music is comforting."	

Key Words

critic *n* a person whose job is to say if art, music, and movies are good or bad; **criticize** *v*

sentimental *adj* strongly showing emotions such as love and sadness

technique *n* a way of doing something

Global Listening

1. 🎧 Listen to the introduction of a lecture on art. What do you think the professor will talk about? Check (✓) your predictions. After you have listened to the whole lecture, see if your predictions were right.

The professor will talk about . . .

_____ techniques that Chagall used in his paintings.

_____ his own experiences with art critics.

_____ critics' opinions about Chagall's paintings.

_____ the purpose of Chagall's art.

_____ different paintings that Chagall made.

2. 🎧 Listen to the lecture. Then circle the statement in each pair that expresses the main idea. Check answers as a class.

1. a. Chagall's art is easy to understand and full of hope.
   b. Chagall's art is abstract and difficult to understand.

2. a. Chagall used only abstract techniques in his work.
   b. Chagall used different styles and techniques to create a feeling of fantasy.

3. a. Critics agree that Chagall's work has strong purpose and meaning.
   b. Some critics believe Chagall's art is too sentimental.

4. a. Chagall's work shows war and loss of hope.
   b. Chagall's work expresses love, joy, and beauty.

Marc Chagall.
The Birthday. 1915.
Oil on canvas.

Speakers may use special words and phrases to show certainty, or how sure they are of their opinions.

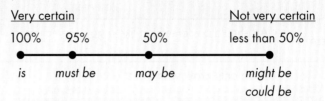

Very certain   Not very certain

100%   95%   50%   less than 50%

is   must be   may be   might be
                                      could be

3. *Listen to the excerpts from the lecture. How certain is the lecturer about each feature of the painting? First, note the words the professor uses to express certainty. Then decide the lecturer's degree of certainty. Compare your answers with a partner's.*

🎧 **Excerpt One:** who the subjects are _____

🎧 **Excerpt Two:** where the subjects' feet are _____

🎧 **Excerpt Three:** where the subjects are _____

Focused Listening

1. 🎧 *Listen to the lecture again. Take notes in the chart with examples from the lecture. Then compare your chart with a partner's.*

Common Themes	Techniques Chagall Used	Experts' Opinions
Modernist art: *social problems,*	*cubist and modernist:*	**Foray:**
		Ott:
Chagall's art:		**Riley:**

2. *Circle the correct answer(s). Use the chart on page 110 to help you.*

1. What is the professor's opinion of *The Birthday?*
   a. It is too sentimental.
   b. It shows Chagall's dreamy joy.
   c. It shows Bella and Chagall.

2. What is Sabina Ott's opinion about Chagall?
   a. His colors are great.
   b. His topics are sentimental.
   c. His paintings are hard to understand.

3. What is Tim Riley's opinion about Chagall?
   a. His art has a real purpose.
   b. His topics are too simple.
   c. His art shows little hope.

Identifying Support for Opinions

Effective speakers and writers support their opinions with reasons or details that are specific, clear, and logical. These may include certain types of details:
- Examples (from personal experience or background)
- Common sense (things everyone knows or can understand)
- Expert evidence (the opinion of experts)
- Statistics (numbers that come from research)

As you read texts or listen to lectures, identify the details that support people's opinions.

3. *Read the statements from the lecture. Opinions are underlined once, and supporting details are underlined twice. Check (✓) the type(s) of support used. Then compare your answers in small groups.*

	Examples	Common Sense	Expert Evidence	Statistics
1. . . . with themes such as love, simple life, and nature, Chagall's art is easy to understand and full of hope.	✓	✓		
2. His [Chagall's] paintings are dreamlike. Look at the painting *The Birthday.* It shows . . .				
3. We know how much he loved Bella, so the man must be Marc and the woman must be Bella.				

(continued on next page)

	Examples	Common Sense	Expert Evidence	Statistics
4. <u>We see a bed and a dresser</u>, so <u>they may be in a bedroom</u>.				
5. . . .his [Chagall's] simple subjects—<u>flying animals and dreamy lovers</u>—make his art too sentimental.				
6. <u>But Chagall's art might have a very important purpose. Art director Tim Riley explains</u> . . .				

4. *Discuss the questions in small groups. Use words to show certainty and provide details to support your opinions.*

1. Do you think Chagall's paintings are too sentimental? Why or why not?

2. Do Chagall's paintings inspire you to look for deeper meaning? Why or why not?

3. What are some other possible purposes of Chagall's paintings? Explain.

4. Chagall said, "Art must be an expression of love or it is nothing." Do you agree or disagree with this statement? Explain.

5. Chagall has been called the "most beloved—and most misunderstood" artist of the twentieth century. Why do you think he has been described this way?

Checkpoint 2 PEARSON LONGMAN myacademicconnectionslab⚓

Before You Speak

Giving and Supporting an Opinion

In academic settings, you may need to state your opinions in discussions, debates, presentations, or papers. When you state your opinions, you must give reasons (facts and examples) to support them. Here are some helpful expressions.

To give an opinion	To support an opinion
I think/believe/feel that . . .	*. . . because . . .*
In my opinion . . .	*. . . for several reasons: . . .*
It seems to me that . . .	

Example

<u>I think that</u> Marc Chagall's painting *The Birthday* is dreamlike, <u>because</u> the people in the picture are flying.

When you give an opinion, use strong support to persuade your audience to agree with you.

• Make sure your ideas are detailed, logical, and clear (easy to understand).

• Use reasons, examples, common sense, expert evidence, or statistics.

• Choose words that show your level of certainty.

4

Building Academic Speaking Skills

In this section, you will practice giving and supporting opinions, and showing agreement and disagreement. Then you will discuss a painting by Marc Chagall.
For online assignments, go to

PEARSON LONGMAN
myacademicconnectionslab

1. Look back at Chagall's paintings on pages 99 and 101. Which do you like better—The Birthday, I and the Village, or neither? Give reasons to support your opinion.

Example

Opinion: *I like the painting* The Birthday *better than the painting* I and the Village.
Reason: *The flying couple gives me a feeling of joy.*

Your Opinion: _____

_____

Reason: _____

_____

Reason: _____

_____

Reason: _____

_____

2. Use your notes from Exercise 1 to write a paragraph expressing and supporting your opinion. Then work with a partner. Evaluate each other's paragraphs. Answer the questions.

1. Does the writer express his or her opinion clearly?   YES   NO

2. Does the writer support his or her opinion with reasons?   YES   NO

3. Is the support detailed, logical, and clear?   YES   NO

If needed, give your partner feedback on how to make the paragraph stronger.

Focused Speaking

Showing Agreement and Disagreement

You can use certain expressions to show agreement or disagreement with someone's opinion.

To show agreement	To show disagreement
I think so, too.	Yes, but . . .
I agree (with you).	I disagree (with you).
I feel the same way.	I see what you mean, but I think . . .
(I think) you're right.	Actually, . . .
That's right/true.	I don't quite agree. What/How about . . . ?

Lyubov Popova.
Lady with the Guitar.
1913–1914. Oil on canvas.

1. 🎧 *Listen to two students discuss Popova's* Lady with the Guitar. *Check (✓) the expressions you hear.*

_____ I think so, too.   _____ I see what you mean, but I think . . .

_____ I agree.   _____ I don't quite agree.

_____ I think you're right.   _____ Yes, but . . .

_____ I feel the same way.   _____ I disagree with you.

_____ That's right.   _____ Actually . . .

2. *Did the speakers agree or disagree about these ideas? Circle* **Agree** *or* **Disagree**.

1. The painting shows a table.	Agree	Disagree
2. The guitar player is wearing a dark shirt or suit.	Agree	Disagree
3. *Lady with the Guitar* shows a strong feeling of sadness.	Agree	Disagree
4. The painting tells the story of a guitar player who lost someone.	Agree	Disagree
5. Popova's *Lady with the Guitar* is cubist.	Agree	Disagree

3. *Discuss the questions with a partner. Use expressions from the skill box on page 113.*

1. Do you agree or disagree with the ideas in Exercise 2?

2. Have your answers to the questions on page 101 about Popova's painting *Lady with the Guitar* changed? If so, how?

4. *Review your notes and paragraph from Exercises 1 and 2 on page 113. In small groups, discuss which Chagall painting you like better—*I and the Village *or* The Birthday. *Use your notes and expressions from the unit to support your opinions and to show agreement and disagreement. You can use these expressions to ask for an opinion:*

- [Name], what do you think about that?
- [Name], what is your opinion?
- How about you, [Name]?

Integrated Speaking Task

You have read a text and listened to a lecture about Marc Chagall's place in modern art, and you have heard a sample discussion about a work of art. You will now use your knowledge of the unit content, topic vocabulary, and fact and opinion to describe and give your opinion about Marc Chagall's painting *Self-Portrait with Seven Fingers* in a group discussion.

Follow the steps to prepare for the discussion.

Step 1: Look at the painting. Complete the chart with facts and opinions about the painting.

Marc Chagall.
Self-Portrait with Seven Fingers. 1913.
Oil on canvas.

What do you see in Chagall's painting, *Self-Portrait with Seven Fingers*? Describe the subject. What themes do you recognize?	
What do you think is the purpose of this painting?	
What similarities/differences do you see between this painting and the others discussed in this unit? In what ways is this painting typical (or not typical) of Chagall's work?	
What personal life experiences do you think may have influenced this painting?	
Do you think the painting is too sentimental or too simple? Explain.	
How do you feel about the painting? Do you like it? Why or why not?	

Step 2: Check (✓) two or three points in the chart in Step 1 that you would like to discuss during the group discussion. Add more details if necessary. You will use your notes during your group discussion.

Step 3: Use the questions from the chart in Step 1 for your small group discussion. Support your opinions with examples. Use the expressions you have learned for giving opinions, agreeing, and disagreeing. Take notes on the discussion in the chart.

	Name: _____	Name: _____	Name: _____	Name: _____
Gave an opinion				
Agreed with an opinion				
Disagreed with an opinion				
Supported an opinion				

Step 4: Evaluate the group discussion. Use the checklist.

Did everyone in your group . . .	Yes	No
give opinions?		
support opinions with examples?		
show agreement and disagreement?		
What did everyone do well in the discussion? _____		

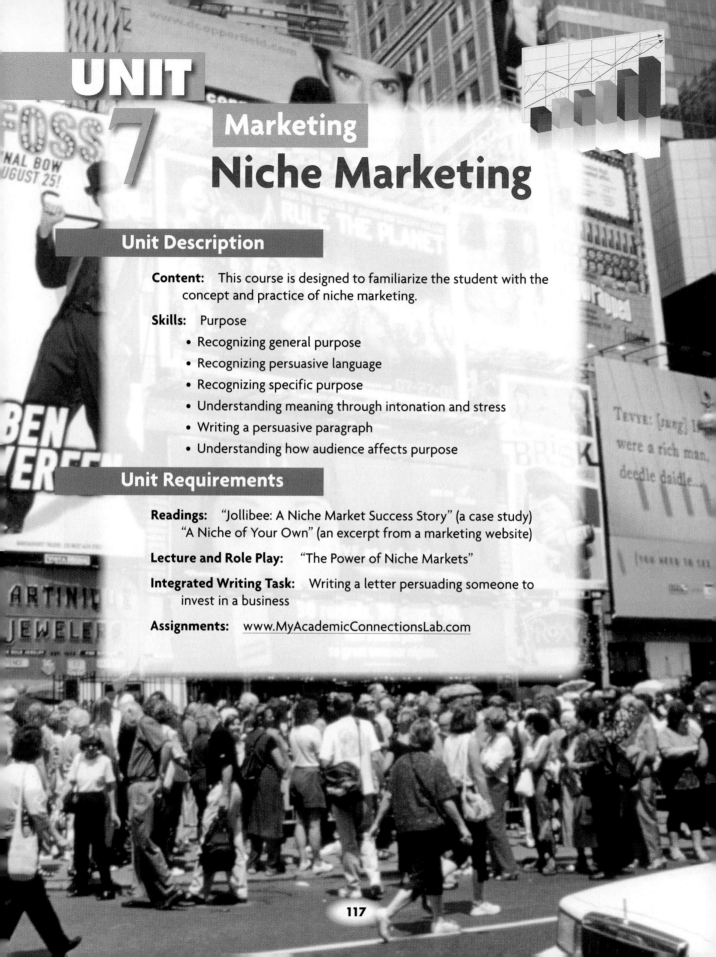

UNIT 7

Marketing
Niche Marketing

Unit Description

Content: This course is designed to familiarize the student with the concept and practice of niche marketing.

Skills: Purpose
- Recognizing general purpose
- Recognizing persuasive language
- Recognizing specific purpose
- Understanding meaning through intonation and stress
- Writing a persuasive paragraph
- Understanding how audience affects purpose

Unit Requirements

Readings: "Jollibee: A Niche Market Success Story" (a case study)
"A Niche of Your Own" (an excerpt from a marketing website)

Lecture and Role Play: "The Power of Niche Markets"

Integrated Writing Task: Writing a letter persuading someone to invest in a business

Assignments: www.MyAcademicConnectionsLab.com

Previewing the Academic Content

Marketing influences what products and services a customer will buy or use. However, since there are so many different kinds of customers and needs, businesses cannot market their products to everyone. As a result, businesses divide markets into specific groups of buyers (for example, by age, family size, marital status, education level, job, nationality, interest, needs, and opinions). Businesses then look at each group and choose the one(s) to which the product will sell the best. Companies often target products to only one small group, or niche market. In this unit, you will look at the benefits of niche marketing and study some examples of niche marketing. You will also look at examples of products sold to niche markets and discuss how a seller can find a niche market for his or her product.

1. *Study the advertisements. Take notes in the chart on page 119. Then discuss the questions with a partner.*

Advertisement A

For the hero in all of us.
Milk's 9 essential nutrients give me the strength and energy I need to fight the forces of evil. Not drinking milk? Now that would be a crime.

got milk?

Advertisement B

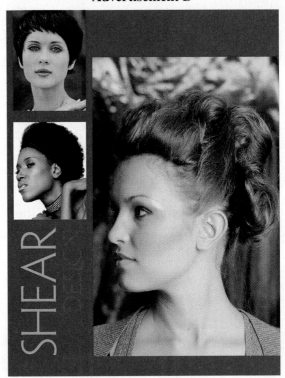

SHEAR

advertise *v* to tell the public about a product or service in order to convince them to buy it; **advertisement** *n*

customer *n* someone who buys things from a store or company

focus on *v* to give all your attention to one particular person or thing

market *n* a specific number or kind of people who want to buy something

market *v* to try to convince someone to buy something by advertising it in a particular way

marketing *n* the activity of deciding how to advertise a product, what price to charge for it, where to sell it, and who to sell it to

niche market *n* a part of the population that buys a particular product or uses a particular service, or is likely to do so; **niche marketing** *n*

target *v* to direct something at someone or something else

	Advertisement A	Advertisement B
What is the product or service?		
Who are the target customers?		
Are you the target market?		

1. What products or services are advertised?

2. Who are probably the target customers for each product or service? Think about the characteristics mentioned in the opening paragraph on page 118 (age, job, etc.) and others you can think of. Be as specific as possible.

3. Do you think you would be part of either advertisers' target market? Why or why not?

2. *List three products or services for which you would be the niche market. Think of your interests and lifestyle. For example, do you play video or computer games? Do you shop at ethnic food markets? Do you need unusually large or small shoes? Discuss your lists in small groups.*

_____

_____

_____

This unit will help you recognize the purpose of readings and lectures. You will also learn how to support your own purpose when writing and speaking.

Previewing the Academic Skills Focus

Purpose is the reason why a speaker says or an author writes something. In this unit, you will learn to recognize two types of purpose: general and specific. A general purpose may be to give information or entertain people with an interesting story. Within the text, there may be information or statements that support the general purpose. The specific purpose of such statements might be to give an example, to show disagreement, or to request information.

1. Match the type of text on the left with the general purpose on the right.

_____ 1. advertisement   a. to entertain

_____ 2. newspaper article   b. to get someone to buy something

_____ 3. novel   c. to give information

2. 🎧 Listen to the classroom conversation between a professor and two students, Lucy and Anthony.

3. 🎧 Listen to the excerpts from the conversation. Match the excerpt on the left with the specific purpose on the right.

_____ 1. Excerpt One (Lucy)   a. to give an example

_____ 2. Excerpt Two (professor)   b. to show agreement

_____ 3. Excerpt Three (Anthony)   c. to request information

_____ 4. Excerpt Four (professor)   d. to show disagreement

Before You Read

1. Work with a partner. Look at the advertisement for Jollibee®, the subject of a marketing case study you will read. Answer the questions on the next page about the ad.

2
Building Academic Reading Skills

In this section, you will learn more about common purposes in academic texts, particularly persuasion. For online assignments, go to

PEARSON LONGMAN
myacademicconnectionslab

Key Words

case study *n* a study of a person, group, situation, or company over a long period of time

compete *v* to try to be more successful than another person or group; **competition** *n*; **competitor** *n*

marketing approach *n* a strategy or way of marketing

persuade *v* to make someone believe or decide to do something

1. What kind of company is Jollibee? What products do you expect them to sell?

2. Who seems to be the likely niche market for Jollibee? What specific customers does the ad target? Explain.

3. What companies might Jollibee compete with? Explain.

2. *Think about a product or service that you used recently and were very satisfied with (for example, a product like clothing or a meal, or a service like a haircut or a sports club membership). Discuss the questions in small groups.*

1. What was the product or service?

2. What persuaded you to try it? For example, did a friend tell you about it? Did you see an ad for the product or service?

3. Do you think that you are part of the target market for this product or service? Why or why not?

4. How does this product or service benefit you? For example, does it save time? Is it useful or helpful? Does it give pleasure? Explain.

Global Reading

Recognizing General Purpose

A **general purpose** is the main reason behind a written or spoken text. It applies to the whole text. These are some common general purposes:

- to persuade (to make someone agree with an opinion or do something)*
- to entertain (to amuse or interest people)
- to narrate (to tell a story)
- to inform (to give information, to teach)*
- to explain (to tell why or how, to give directions)*

* These purposes are common in academic texts.

Use these skimming strategies to recognize the purpose of a written text:

- Quickly read the title and introductory sentence or paragraph. The writer's purpose may be directly stated there.
- Look at pictures and charts. These are often included to inform or to explain.
- Notice the type of supporting details. Facts are often used to inform or to explain. Opinions are often given to persuade.
- Look at the quotations included. Do they support a specific opinion or general information?

1. *Skim Part A of the text—the Case Study section of a marketing class website—for one minute. Think about the general purpose(s) of the text.*

Part A

MKTG 101: Niche Marketing

ASSIGNMENTS

DISCUSSION BOARD

SUBJECT: Reading Assignment 4: Case Study
POSTED BY: Professor Kline, March 12, 7:56 A.M.

Welcome to the online portion of our class. Please read the case study, "Jollibee: A Niche Market Success Story," and post your responses to the online discussion board.

Tony Tan Caktiong, Founder of Jollibee

CASE STUDY: Jollibee: A Niche Market Success Story

1   When someone says "fast food restaurant," most people will think of McDonald's. However, if someone said the same words in the Philippines, most people would think of Jollibee. Jollibee isn't famous around the world like McDonald's. But in its niche—the Philippines—Jollibee is the number-one fast food place, with 1,414 restaurants. In the Philippines, Jollibee makes twice as much money as McDonald's.

2   Jollibee's story began in 1975, when Tony Tan Caktiong started two ice cream shops in the Philippines. After he saw the success that McDonald's was having around the world, he turned his shops into fast food restaurants. Tan Caktiong explained his method of marketing: "We felt that we could not compete with McDonald's. Therefore, we targeted a niche market. We targeted Filipinos." More specifically, Jollibee targeted Filipino families who love their culture and want a happy family experience when they go out.

3   To attract these customers, Jollibee decided to focus on three things: Filipino taste, traditional Filipino families, and creating a fun place to go. First, Tan Caktiong wanted to serve special food that Filipinos like: rice or noodles instead of French fries, fruity desserts, and sweet, spicy burgers. In fact, the Jollibee Yumburger is similar to what a Filipino mother would cook at home. As seen from its success, Jollibee understands Filipino taste and culture well.

4   Tan Caktiong also made sure that Filipinos would see Jollibee as a place for families. For example, in a well-known TV ad, Filipino actor Aga Muhlach and his wife and two children enjoy a Jollibee meal together. This is exactly what you see when you enter a Jollibee restaurant: happy families eating together.

5   Finally, Tan Caktiong wanted to create a fun dining experience. This is characterized by a special character: a smiling, colorful bee that children love. Tan Caktiong chose this character, and the name Jollibee, because the jolly—or happy—bee jumps around and enjoys the good things in life.

6   Clearly, Jollibee has shown it can compete with the world's biggest fast food restaurant—McDonald's—by recognizing and understanding its target market and by giving its customers exactly what they want.

Source: Adapted from Kotler, P., & Armostrong, G. (2006). *Principles of marketing* (11th ed). Upper Saddle River, NJ: Pearson Prentice Hall.

2. The two general purposes of the case study are to inform students about Jollibee and to explain how it is a successful example of niche marketing. Work with a partner. Underline three pieces of information from the text in Part A that show these purposes.

3. Skim Part B of the text—the Student Response section of the class website—for one minute. Work with a partner. Identify the general purpose of the student paragraph (see the skill box on page 121). Underline any information from the paragraph that shows this purpose. Discuss your choices with the class.

Part B

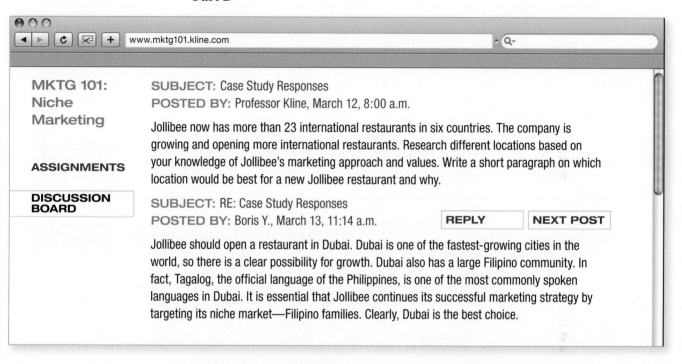

4. Read both Part A and Part B. Then work in groups of four. Each person should choose one question and write a main idea statement to answer the question. When done, each person shares the main idea statements with the group. Decide together if each person answered his or her question completely and correct the statements as needed.

1. Who did Jollibee target?

_____

2. What did Jollibee do to attract its customers?

_____

3. How was Jollibee able to compete with a large international company?

_____

4. Where does the student think Jollibee should open a restaurant?

_____

Focused Reading

1. *Read the text again. Then read the sentences from the text in the chart. Write details to support each statement. Then scan the text to check your answers.*

Excerpt	Supporting Details
1. In its niche—the Philippines—Jollibee is the number-one fast food place . . .	
2. [Jollibee] targeted a niche market.	
3. Tan Caktiong wanted to serve special food that Filipinos like.	
4. Tan Caktiong wanted to create a fun dining experience.	
5. Jollibee should open a restaurant in Dubai.	

Recognizing Persuasive Language

The use of persuasive language is very common in academic settings. Writers and speakers use special expressions to persuade their audience to think about a topic in a certain way or to take action. These expressions show that the writer or speaker believes a statement to be correct or very important:

> *Obviously, . . .*
> *Clearly, . . .*
> *It is important / essential / necessary . . .*
> *should / must / need to*
> *I strongly believe . . .*
> *I am confident (that) . . .*

2. *Scan the text and circle the persuasive expressions. Then discuss the questions with the class.*

1. Why does the student paragraph use a high level of persuasion?

2. Why do you usually not see a high level of persuasion in textbooks or professors' materials, such as the case study?

3. *Discuss the questions in small groups. Use persuasive language.*

1. What is the most important reason for Jollibee's success? Why?

2. Which would be a better location for a Jollibee restaurant—a big city with a small, strong Filipino community, or a suburb where many families live but most are not Filipino? Explain.

3. Would your city be a good choice for a Jollibee restaurant? Why or why not?

Checkpoint 1 PEARSON LONGMAN myacademicconnectionslab

Before You Listen

1. *Read the advice from marketing experts. Then paraphrase it starting with the phrase* You should . . . . *Write in your notebook.*

> 1. Know your market before you start your business.
>   **EXAMPLE:** *You should understand your customers before beginning a company.*
> 2. Stress how your service is different.
> 3. Evaluate your budget.
> 4. Use a niche marketing approach when your company resources[1] are limited.
> 5. Know your target customer groups so well that you meet their needs better than other businesses.
>
> _____
> [1] **resources** *n* all the money, skills, etc. that you have available to use
>
> Source: Items 1 and 2 adapted from Brotsky, B. (1992). *Finding your niche: marketing your professional service.* Berkeley, CA: Community Resource Institute Press. Items 3–5 adapted from Kotler, P., & Armostrong, G. (2006). *Principles of marketing* (11th ed). Upper Saddle River, NJ: Pearson Prentice Hall.

2. *Circle the correct answers to complete the paragraph.*

When (1) ***expanding / consulting*** with businesses on the benefits of niche marketing, it is useful to give examples of successful businesses that have used this method of marketing. Apple Inc. is one great example. Instead of competing with PC makers that offer cheap computers to a large group of customers, Apple (2) ***specializes / expands*** in specific products for a more

(continued on next page)

Building Academic Listening Skills

In this section, you will practice recognizing the purpose of specific statements. You will also learn how speakers use intonation and stress to express meaning. For online assignments, go to

PEARSON LONGMAN myacademicconnectionslab

consult *v* to provide information, advice, or answers; **consultant** *n*

expand *v* to become or make something larger in size or amount

limited *adj* not very great in amount or number; **limit** *v*

profit *n* money that you gain by selling things or doing business

specialize *v* to limit most of your business or study to a specific group, subject, etc. **specialized** *adj*

(3) *limited / expanding* market. For example, when it introduced iTunes, it made a large (4) *consultant / profit* because other businesses were not serving the needs of customers who wanted to buy music online. After its success with iTunes, Apple (5) *expanded / consulted* its profit with other tools, such as the iPhone.

3. *You will listen to a lecture and role play. The title of the lecture is* The Power of Niche Marketing. *Based on the title, what do you predict is the general purpose of the lesson?*

Global Listening

1. ⌒ *Listen to the lecture and role play. Take notes on the main ideas.*

2. *Read the statements. Decide if they are true or false. Write **T** (true) or **F** (false). Use your notes. Then check your answers with a partner.*

_____ 1. The goal of niche marketing is to serve a large part of the market that most competitors don't serve.

_____ 2. Before expanding, businesses should become successful in a market niche.

_____ 3. When a business knows who has the biggest need for its product, it can fill these customers' needs better.

_____ 4. If a small business tries to attract a large market right away, it will probably run out of customers.

Recognizing Specific Purpose

A speaker or writer's **specific purpose** is his or her reason for making a specific statement or including certain information. Much of the specific information a speaker or writer includes will support the general purpose, so recognizing specific purpose can help you understand important ideas.

These are some common specific purposes:

- to give an example or to illustrate a point
- to show agreement or disagreement
- to request information
- to emphasize or show the importance of a point

A specific purpose may be stated directly. If it is not, you can ask these questions to recognize it:

- Why is the speaker (or writer) making this statement or including this information?
- What does the speaker (or writer) want the audience (the listeners or readers) to do?

3. *Read the questions. Then listen to three excerpts from the lecture and check (✓) the specific purpose of each statement. Make a note of any clues that helped you recognize the purpose.*

🎧 Excerpt One

1. What is the purpose of the teaching assistant's response to the "consultant"?

_____ to give an example/illustrate a point

_____ to show agreement

_____ to show disagreement

_____ to request information

✓ to emphasize or show the importance of a point

Clues: *"but still," stress on "really," repeats earlier statement*

🎧 Excerpt Two

2. Why does the teaching assistant say, "Yes, that's exactly right"?

_____ to give an example/illustrate a point

_____ to show agreement

_____ to show disagreement

_____ to request information

_____ to emphasize or show the importance of a point

Clues: _____

3. Why does the teaching assistant repeat the definition of *niche marketing*?

_____ to give an example/illustrate a point

_____ to show agreement

_____ to show disagreement

_____ to request information

_____ to emphasize or show the importance of a point

Clues: _____

🎧 Excerpt Three

4. Why does Park mention Jollibee?

_____ to give an example/illustrate a point

_____ to show agreement

_____ to show disagreement

_____ to request information

_____ to emphasize or show the importance of a point

Clues: _____

4. Discuss your answers to Exercise 3 with the class. Did the same clues help you to recognize the specific purposes?

Focused Listening

1. ⌒ Listen to the lecture again. Complete the statements with the words from the box.

buyers	Jollibee	large	limited	need	successful

1. Big companies may not serve a certain part of the market because it is not

   _____ enough for them to make a profit.

2. Many small businesses want to serve all customers even when they have a

   _____ amount of money.

3. Small business owners sometimes fear that if they focus on only one group

   of _____, they won't make enough of a profit.

4. A small business owner should always find out who has the biggest

   _____ for his or her product.

5. _____ is an example of a business that started small and

   grew bigger after becoming _____.

Understanding Meaning through Intonation and Stress

To express ideas clearly, speakers often use intonation and stress to give clues about their meaning.

Intonation is the rising ↑ and falling ↓ of your voice. Speakers can use intonation to show the meaning of a word or statement. Intonation often rises when someone is happy, excited, asking a question, or joking in a positive way. Intonation often falls when someone is upset, serious, or joking in a negative way.

⌒ **Examples:**

Twenty-five dollars for a meal! ↑ (Meaning: The meal is probably great and doesn't cost a lot.)

Twenty-five dollars for a meal! ↓ (Meaning: The meal costs too much.)

Stress is putting extra emphasis on certain words—for example, by saying them more loudly or slowly. A statement can have different meanings depending on which word is stressed.

⌒ **Examples:**

We saw a <u>funny</u> advertisement. (The ad wasn't sad or serious.)

We <u>saw</u> a funny advertisement. (We didn't hear the ad. We saw it.)

<u>We</u> saw a funny advertisement. (We saw the ad, but you didn't.)

2. *Listen for intonation and stress in the excerpts from the lecture. For each item, mark the rising ↑ and falling ↓ intonation, and underline any words that are stressed. Then circle the correct meaning.*

🎧 **Excerpt One:** Any volunteers? Anyone at all? ↑ Don't <u>all</u> offer at once.
   a. There are too many volunteers.
   (b.) No one is offering to volunteer.

🎧 **Excerpt Two:** OK, now, when you're out in the real world, let's say consulting with clients, you'll quickly realize that many small businesses want to serve everyone, even with a limited amount of money for marketing.
   a. School isn't like the world of business.
   b. Many students have jobs outside of class.

🎧 **Excerpt Three:** Plus, who doesn't like ice cream?
   a. The speaker wants to find out who doesn't like his product.
   b. The speaker thinks everyone likes his product.

🎧 **Excerpt Four:** Well, how many millions of dollars do you have to market your product to the world?
   a. The speaker knows his client doesn't have enough money.
   b. The speaker wonders how much money his client has to spend.

🎧 **Excerpt Five:** Ah-ha. I see what you're saying. I need to think about who really wants my ice cream.
   a. The speaker finally understands.
   b. The speaker disagrees.

3. 🎧 *Listen for stress in an excerpt from the lecture. Circle the correct answers.*

1. Which word does the speaker stress in the following statement? *You can't do that.*
   a. you
   b. can't

2. What does the speaker mean?
   a. That could work for a big business, but not for you.
   b. You are not allowed to do this.

3. If the speaker wanted to show that the client could do something else, which word would he probably have stressed?
   a. do
   b. that

4. *Work in groups of three. Your company has developed a new breakfast product. Your team's job is to find a niche market for the product and to persuade the company to focus on this niche. This is called* pitching. *Follow the steps.*

Step 1: Choose a product.
- Fruit drink with vitamins targeted for weight loss
- Breakfast bar in the shape of a popular children's cartoon character
- Egg sandwich with vegetables
- (your own idea) _____

Step 2: Choose the best niche market for your product. Make a list of the characteristics of people who probably want this product. Discuss why your product is important to your target customers and how it can help them.

Step 3: Write your pitch. Answer this question: **What is the best niche market for this product, and why?** Include a description of your product and give strong reasons to support your opinion. Use persuasive expressions from page 124.

Step 4: Pitch your idea to the class. Divide the tasks among group members.
- Introduce your product and niche market.
- Describe your niche market.
- Give reasons for your choice of niche market.

Checkpoint 2   PEARSON LONGMAN **myacademicconnectionslab**

4

Building Academic Writing Skills

In this section, you will practice writing persuasive paragraphs. Then you will use ideas and vocabulary from this unit to write a letter to persuade an investor to invest in a business. For online assignments, go to

PEARSON LONGMAN
myacademicconnectionslab

Before You Write

Writing a Persuasive Paragraph

The goal of a persuasive paragraph is to convince the audience to take an action or to think about something in a certain way. In a persuasive paragraph:

- The **topic sentence** (main idea) usually gives the writer's opinion. It may give his or her purpose directly.
- The **body of the paragraph** includes facts, quotations, and examples that support the writer's opinion. All of these details relate to the main idea.
- The **concluding sentence** either calls the reader to take a specific action or repeats the topic sentence in different words.

1. *Work with a partner. Look again at the persuasive student paragraph on the website on page 123. Complete the tasks.*

1. Underline the topic sentence once. What main idea does it introduce?

2. What facts, quotations, or examples does the student give? Do they all relate to the main idea?

3. Underline the concluding sentence twice. Does this sentence call the reader to take a specific action, or does it repeat the topic sentence in different words?

2. *Susan van der Kamp is looking for someone to invest[1] in her business selling stroopwafels—Dutch cookies—to coffee and tea shops in New Zealand. Read her letter. Later, you will choose a persuasive paragraph to complete the letter.*

Stroopwafels are popular Dutch cookies filled with a sweet syrup

1011 Sutherland Road
Wellington 6023

August 18, 2009

Steven Wong, CEO
Wong and Associates
P.O. Box 5690
Wellington 6015

Dear Mr. Wong:

My name is Susan van der Kamp, and I am starting a stroopwafel business in New Zealand. Stroopwafels are popular cookies in the Netherlands. They are delicious when put on top of a hot drink to warm the syrup inside of them. I have developed a strong plan to make my business a success, and I am inviting you to invest in it.

(persuasive paragraph goes here)

After you have looked over my marketing plan, I would like to discuss the opportunity for you to invest in this unique business.

Sincerely,

Susan van der Kamp

Susan van der Kamp

---

[1] **invest** *v* to give money to a company, business, or bank in order to get a profit later on

3. *Read the two paragraphs. Both paragraphs try to persuade investor Steven Wong to support Susan van der Kamp's business. As you read each paragraph, complete the tasks. Think about which paragraph Ms. van der Kamp should use in her letter. Complete the tasks.*

- Circle persuasive language.
- Underline the topic sentence (if any) once.
- Note the details in the body of the paragraph and how they relate to the main idea.
- Underline the concluding sentence (if any) twice.

Paragraph A

I think that my stroopwafel business might be a good investment opportunity for you. Like other successful businesses that have used niche marketing, I have chosen to focus on a small market—Dutch immigrants in New Zealand. There are more than 140,000 people of Dutch descent[1] here. My plan is to sell stroopwafels to local coffee shops and tearooms in Wellington, where there is a large Dutch population. Soon I plan to take my business to other parts of New Zealand.

---

[1] **descent** *n* family origins, especially nationality or relationship to someone important who lived a long time ago

Paragraph B

I am confident that my stroopwafel business will succeed here, because there is already an interested group of buyers for my product. As a successful restaurant investor, you must know about Jollibee and its marketing approach of focusing on Filipino communities. Like Jollibee, I have decided to focus on a small niche, Dutch immigrants in New Zealand. This market is specific but strong—more than 140,000 people. Non-Dutch people also enjoy this treat. In fact, even Starbucks now sells stroopwafels at their shops in the United States. My plan is to sell stroopwafels to local coffee shops and tearooms in Wellington, where there is already a large Dutch population. Later I plan to expand my business to other parts of New Zealand. I strongly believe that my stroopwafel business would be a very profitable investment for you.

4. *Work with a partner. Compare the notes you took while reading. Which paragraph is more persuasive? What makes this paragraph more persuasive? Be specific.*

Focused Writing

1. *Read the advice from marketing entrepreneur Bob Leduc on how businesses can find their niche markets. Underline the most important ideas. Then work with a partner. Discuss the most important ideas of the excerpt. What is its general purpose?*

A Niche of Your Own: *Finding a Niche Market*
by Bob Leduc

1. First, list all the benefits that your product or service gives. For example, a product might save time, save money, or give pleasure.
2. List some of the characteristics of customers who would benefit from your product.
3. Decide if the group you've identified is profitable and if you can connect with it. If so, you should be able to answer YES to these questions:

   ■ Do your target customers have a strong need for your product or service?

   ■ Do they have money to pay for your product or service?

   ■ Is this group big enough to give you enough business?

   ■ Can you find ways to reach your niche through marketing and ads?

   ■ Can you clearly explain your product/service to these customers and persuade them of its benefits?

If you answer YES to all these questions, you've found a successful niche market!

Source: Adapted from Leduc, B. (1999). Target a niche market to increase your sales and profits. Retrieved May 27, 2009, from http://www.soho.org/Marketing-Articles/Target-a-Niche.htm.

Understanding How Audience Affects Purpose

When preparing to write or speak, think about your audience—the people you are writing or speaking to. Understanding your audience can influence your purpose and affect how you present information. To help identify your audience, think about these questions:

• Who will be your readers? (children, men, students, parents, etc.)
• What do you know about them? (gender, interests, feelings toward topic, education level, etc.)

Use what you know about your audience to identify your own purpose and to choose the best techniques for sharing information. Here are some examples:

• If your audience has opinions that are different from yours, you may try to persuade them.
• If your audience has little knowledge of your subject, you may need to inform them about it or explain it to them.
• If your audience has little interest in your subject, it may be helpful to entertain them as you give information.

2. *Answer the questions. Discuss your ideas with the class.*

1. Look again at Leduc's advice on page 133. Who is probably his audience? How do you know?

2. What suggestions would you give Leduc on how to present this information if his audience:
   - Knew nothing about niche marketing?
   - Wasn't interested in this topic?

Integrated Writing Task

You have read texts and listened to a lecture about niche marketing. You will now use your knowledge of the unit content, topic vocabulary, purpose, persuasive language, and audience to write a letter persuading someone to invest in a business.

Follow the steps to write your letter.

Step 1: Choose a product or service that interests you (for example, a health product or a type of entertainment or work you can provide). Imagine that you are a small business owner marketing this product.

Step 2: You will write a letter to Julia Pinto, a young investor who works with small, local businesses. Your purpose is to inform her about your business and persuade her to invest in it. Answer the questions to provide information about your business. Take notes in your notebook.

1. What is your business? What product or service do you provide?

2. Why is your business a good investment? How will a niche marketing approach help it succeed?

3. Use Leduc's advice to find a niche market. Describe the specific characteristics of your target market. Why is this market strong?

4. Consider Jollibee's niche marketing approach. What is one example or connection with Jollibee that you can use to persuade your investor?

Step 3: Use your notes to make a paragraph outline. Use the skills box on page 130 as a checklist. In your topic sentence, give your opinion about why your business will be successful and why it is a good investment opportunity. See Paragraph B on page 132 for an example.

Step 4: Use your outline to write a persuasive paragraph. Use persuasive language and some of the expressions to make connections between your marketing plan and important ideas and examples in this unit.
- *I have chosen to focus on a small niche market because . . .*
- *I believe the market I have chosen is strong because . . .*
- *You've probably heard about the success of Jollibee . . .*
- *Like Jollibee, . . .*

Step 5: Complete the letter. Then add your persuasive paragraph.

_____
(your street)

_____
(your city, state, and postal code)

_____
(today's date)

Julia Pinto
Pinto Investment Group
771 Commonwealth Avenue
Boston, MA 02116

Dear Ms. Pinto:

My name is _____ , and I am starting
(your name)

a business that will provide _____
(product/service)

_____ . I am inviting you to invest in

this business, which I'm confident will be a great success.

(add your paragraph)

_____

_____

_____

_____

_____

_____

_____

_____

I will contact you again soon to see if you are interested in investing in this
opportunity, and to answer any questions you have.

Sincerely,

_____
(your signature)

_____
(your name)

Step 6: Exchange your letter with a partner. Comment on your partner's persuasive paragraph. Use the checklist.

Paragraph Checklist	Yes	No
Does the topic sentence give an opinion?		
Does the body . . . • include facts, quotations, and examples that support the writer's opinion? • have details that relate to the main idea?		
Does the concluding sentence . . . • call the reader to take a specific action? • repeat the topic sentence in different words?		

Step 7: Revise your paragraph based on your partner's comments.

Step 8: Work in small groups. Imagine that you work for Ms. Pinto's investment company. Read and discuss each letter. Choose one business to support. Share and explain your choice with the class.

Communication
Nonverbal Communication

Unit Description

Content: This course is designed to familiarize the student with the concept of nonverbal communication.

Skills: Inference

- Making inferences about a speaker's attitude
- Inferring word meaning from context
- Presenting a role play
- Using stress, intonation, and pauses to express meaning

Unit Requirements

Lecture and Discussion: "Nonverbal Communication: Uses and Misunderstandings"

Readings: "Studies in nonverbal communication" (a student summary)

"Proxemics for Better Communication" (an excerpt from a scientific journal)

Integrated Speaking Task: Preparing and participating in a role play demonstrating nonverbal communication

Assignments: www.MyAcademicConnectionsLab.com

1

Preview

For online assignments, go to

PEARSON LONGMAN
myacademicconnectionslab

Key Words

attitude *n* a general opinion or feeling about someone or something

communication *n* the process of sharing information or expressing thoughts and feelings; **communicate** *v*

complex *adj* consisting of many different parts and often difficult to understand

interpret *v* to explain or determine the meaning of a statement, action, event, etc.; **interpretation** *n*

misunderstanding *n* a failure to comprehend a question, statement, or situation; **misunderstand** *v*

tone of voice *n* the way your voice sounds, which often shows how you are feeling or what you mean

Previewing the Academic Content

The process of sending and receiving messages without words is called *nonverbal communication*. Nonverbal communication includes the use of the body, face, and tone of voice to express meaning. This element of communication is central to how people understand and relate to one another. Each day people send and receive thousands of nonverbal messages. Nonverbal communication is also complex, as people interpret nonverbal messages based on their own culture and background.

In this unit, you will study elements of nonverbal communication and how important nonverbal clues are in everday communication. You will also learn some universal ways in which people use nonverbal communication. Finally, you will look at issues or misunderstandings that can happen when people interpret nonverbal messages.

1. *Read the paragraph about a study by psychologist Albert Mehrabian and study the pie chart showing Mehrabian's findings. Then discuss the questions on page 139 with the class.*

Albert Mehrabian is a psychologist known for his studies of the relationship between verbal and nonverbal communication. Mehrabian found that face-to-face communication has three basic elements: words, tone of voice, and nonverbal messages. He also found that nonverbal messages are especially important in communicating feelings and attitudes. According to his study, when a person's words express a different attitude or feeling than the nonverbal messages he or she gives, people are more likely to believe the nonverbal messages.

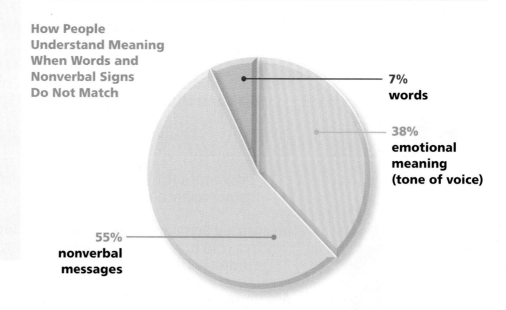

How People Understand Meaning When Words and Nonverbal Signs Do Not Match

7% **words**

38% **emotional meaning (tone of voice)**

55% **nonverbal messages**

Source: Adapted from Mehrabian, A. (1981). *Silent messages: Implicit communication of emotions and attitudes.* Belmont, CA: Wadsworth.

1. How much meaning is expressed through words when those words seem to be different from nonverbal signals? How much meaning is expressed through nonverbal communication?

2. Do these findings surprise you? Explain.

2. *Look at the photo of two people. What attitudes and feelings does each person show? Write **W** for the woman, **M** for the man, or **B** for both. Some of the choices may not be correct for either person. Use a dictionary if needed.*

_____ aggressive	_____ helpful	_____ relaxed	_____ understanding
_____ angry	_____ humorous	_____ sad	_____ upset
_____ frustrated	_____ offended	_____ sorry	_____ (others): _____
_____ happy	_____ persuasive	_____ uncomfortable	

3. *Discuss your answers to Exercise 2 in small groups. Answer the questions.*

1. Which attitudes and feelings did you choose?

2. How did the people's bodies, hands, and faces help you understand their feelings?

3. What do you think is happening in this situation? What do you think the people are saying? Do their nonverbal messages match what you think they are saying?

This unit will help you understand ideas and attitudes that are not stated directly. It will also show you how to express your own ideas, meanings, and attitudes using stress, intonation, and pauses.

Previewing the Academic Skills Focus

Inference

Writers and speakers do not always state their meaning, purpose, or feelings directly. They often **imply**, or suggest, these things by giving certain types of clues. The reader or listener must look for these clues and put together all the information given to **infer**, or guess, the meaning, purpose, and feelings.

To **make inferences**, look for these types of clues:

- Content: What facts or information are included or not included?
- Word choice: What attitudes or opinions does the choice of words show?
- Intonation or stress (for speakers only): How does the speaker say something? What does this show?

To check your inference, ask, "How do I know the writer (or speaker) meant this?"

1. *Make inferences to understand the cartoon. Work with a partner to answer the questions.*

1. Where are the two men? What do you think people do at this place?

2. Who are the two men? How are they dressed? How old are they?

3. What is happening in the cartoon? What are the men doing? What meaning and feelings do their actions express? Explain.

4. How do the men feel about each other? How do you know?

2. 🎧 *Listen to and make inferences about a comment made by a student from a class on nonverbal communication. Take notes to answer the questions. Then compare your answers with a partner's.*

1. What is the student's purpose for sharing this information? What specific facts or information does she include to communicate this purpose?

2. How does the student feel? Which words show this? Does she use stress or intonation to show her feelings? If so, how?

2

Building Academic Listening Skills

In this section, you will learn more about using information you hear to make inferences.
For online assignments, go to

myacademicconnectionslab

Key Words

appropriate *adj* correct or good for a particular time, situation, or purpose

assume *v* to think that something is true even though you do not know that it is; **assumption** *n*

gesture *n* a movement of your head, arm, or hand to express your feeling

potential *n* the possibility that something will develop or happen in a particular way

regulate *v* to control an activity or process, usually by having rules

signal *n* a sound, action, or event that gives information or tells someone to do something

Before You Listen

Kinesics is a type of nonverbal communication that studies gestures—movements of the body. Work in small groups. Answer the questions about gestures. Use the key words in your discussion.

1. Look at the gesture that means "I don't know" in Western cultures. Do you know of any other meanings for this gesture? Do you know of any other gestures that signal the same thing? What are they?

2. Do you know any gestures to communicate these ideas? If so, show them to your partner.

Good job!	No way!	Watch out!	Pay attention!
Who? Me?	Good-bye.	Come here.	

3. Do you think gestures mean the same thing in every culture? Explain.

4. Do you know of any gestures that are appropriate in one culture or situation but not in another? Explain.

Global Listening

1. 🎧 *Listen to the lecture and group discussion. Take notes on the main ideas.*

2. *Read the statements. Decide if they are true or false. Write **T** (true) or **F** (false). Use your notes. Then compare your answers with a partner's.*

_____ 1. Not all cultures use nonverbal communication.

_____ 2. One way people use nonverbal communication is to regulate conversation.

_____ 3. A gesture is specific intonation that communicates an idea.

_____ 4. Nonverbal signals are an effective way to communicate across cultures.

_____ 5. Ai's (the Japanese student's) experience is an example of how nonverbal signals are used to take turns speaking.

3. Review the skill box on page 140. Then listen to the excerpts from the lecture and the discussion, and circle the correct answer to complete each statement. For each statement, note specific words or other clues (content, intonation and stress, or word choice) that helped you infer the answer.

Excerpt One (Professor)

1. The professor wants students *to use / to understand the use of* gestures across cultures.

   Notes: _____

2. The professor suggests that people *can / cannot* change their communication style when needed.

   Notes: _____

Excerpt Two (Ai Sato)

3. The student implies that in Japanese culture it is not polite to *be quiet / talk too much* in conversation.

   Notes: _____

4. The student suggests that Japanese and American cultures use *different / the same* nonverbal signals to regulate conversation.

   Notes: _____

Excerpt Three (Ai Sato)

5. The student would *disagree / agree* with the idea that people can change their nonverbal communication styles when needed.

   Notes: _____

Excerpt Four (Tim White)

6. The student's general purpose is to *entertain / inform* his classmates with a personal example.

   Notes: _____

Focused Listening

1. Listen again to the lecture and the discussion. Answer the questions in small groups.

1. What are two examples of how people in Western cultures show they want a turn to speak in conversation?

2. According to the professor, what is one example of a gesture?

3. According to Tim White, what are two examples of how his classmate is rude?

An attitude is how someone generally feels or thinks about something. Speakers often do not directly state their attitudes. In this case, the listener must listen carefully for specific clues that suggest what the speaker is feeling. To make inferences about a speaker's attitude, listen for:

- The speaker's word choices. Words like *good* or *best* show a positive attitude, while words like *bad* or *wrong* show a negative attitude. Also, certain words make an idea stronger—for example, *very, really, so,* and *just.*

- Stress. A speaker may emphasize words to show strong feelings.

  ∩ **Example**
      No.
      NO!

- Intonation. Speakers often use rising intonation to show positive feelings and falling intonation to show negative feelings.

  ∩ **Example**
      "Good morning!" (rising intonation)
      "Good morning." (falling intonation)

2. *Read the words. Decide if their meaning shows a positive or negative attitude. Write **+** for positive and **−** for negative. Use a dictionary if needed.*

__−__ 1. but	_____ 6. good	_____ 11. rude
_____ 2. comfortable	_____ 7. hard	_____ 12. too much
_____ 3. difficult	_____ 8. help	_____ 13. trouble
_____ 4. enough	_____ 9. polite	_____ 14. uncomfortable
_____ 5. fine	_____ 10. problem	_____ 15. yes

3. *Listen to the excerpts from the lecture and the discussion. Listen for stress, intonation, and word choice to infer attitude. Write **+** for positive or **−** for negative to show the general attitude expressed in each excerpt. Then use the words from the box to complete the statements describing each speaker's feeling or attitude. You can use more than one word for each statement.*

confident	frustrated	helpful	offended	relaxed	uncomfortable	upset

∩ **Excerpt One**

general attitude: _____

Ai Sato used to feel _____ when she first had conversations with Americans.

(continued on next page)

⌒ Excerpt Two

general attitude: _____

Ai Sato now feels _____ speaking with Americans.

⌒ Excerpt Three

general attitude: _____

Tim White feels _____ by his classmate who tries to answer all of the teacher's questions.

⌒ Excerpt Four

general attitude: _____

The professor is _____ when he tells the students to be careful with gestures.

4. *In your notebook, write a paragraph about a misunderstanding you have experienced due to nonverbal communication. Include specific examples. Then share your experiences in small groups.*

Checkpoint 1   PEARSON LONGMAN **myacademicconnectionslab**

Before You Read

1. *Work with a partner. Take turns talking for 60 seconds about what you are going to do after class today. Then answer the questions.*

1. During how much of your conversation did you look at each other—for more than half or less than half of the time?

2. Did you look at your partner more when you were speaking or when you were listening?

3. What percentage of the time do you think people look at one another during a conversation?

2. *Read the textbook paragraph. Then discuss the questions on page 145 with your partner.*

Then discuss the questions on page 145 with your partner.

> Gaze is when, where, and how long a person looks at someone else. This includes eye contact—when two people look directly at one another. Michael Argyle and Mark Cook (1976) studied gaze during conversations of English-speaking people and had these results:
>
> ■ Listeners gaze at speakers 70 percent of the time.
> ■ Speakers gaze at their listeners 40 percent of the time.
> ■ Speakers and listeners share eye contact with each other 30 percent of the time.
>
> Argyle, M., & Cook, M. (1976). *Gaze and mutual gaze.* New York: Cambridge University Press.

3
Building Academic Reading Skills

In this section, you will learn how to infer the meaning of new vocabulary, and you will practice making inferences based on information you read. For online assignments, go to

PEARSON LONGMAN
myacademicconnectionslab

1. Look at your notes from Exercise 1. Was your experience similar to or different from Argyle and Cook's findings?

2. Do you think the results of the study would be the same or different in your culture? Explain.

3. In what situations is it appropriate and inappropriate to gaze at another person in your culture? How is this different from other cultures you know of?

Key Words

analyze *v* to look at or think about the parts of something in order to understand the whole thing

calm down *v* to become quiet and relaxed after you have been angry, excited, or upset, or to make someone become quiet and relaxed; **calm** *adj*

method *n* a planned way of doing something

Global Reading

1. *Read the student summary and classmates' comments from the website of an online communications class. Underline the main ideas. (Do not use a dictionary for new words. Later you will infer their meaning.)*

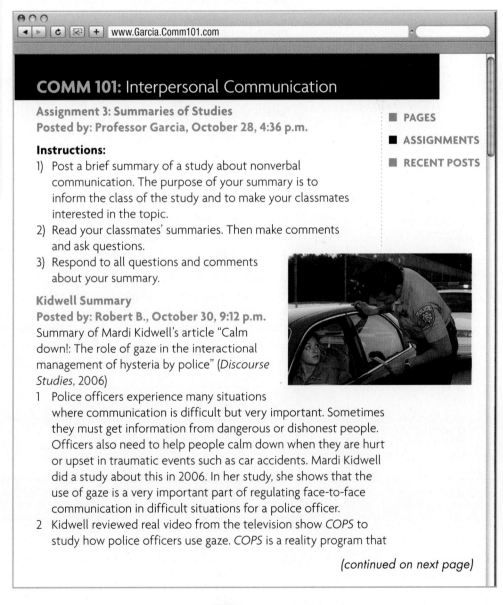

www.Garcia.Comm101.com

COMM 101: Interpersonal Communication

Assignment 3: Summaries of Studies
Posted by: Professor Garcia, October 28, 4:36 p.m.

■ PAGES
■ ASSIGNMENTS
■ RECENT POSTS

Instructions:

1) Post a brief summary of a study about nonverbal communication. The purpose of your summary is to inform the class of the study and to make your classmates interested in the topic.

2) Read your classmates' summaries. Then make comments and ask questions.

3) Respond to all questions and comments about your summary.

Kidwell Summary
Posted by: Robert B., October 30, 9:12 p.m.
Summary of Mardi Kidwell's article "Calm down!: The role of gaze in the interactional management of hysteria by police" (*Discourse Studies*, 2006)

1   Police officers experience many situations where communication is difficult but very important. Sometimes they must get information from dangerous or dishonest people. Officers also need to help people calm down when they are hurt or upset in traumatic events such as car accidents. Mardi Kidwell did a study about this in 2006. In her study, she shows that the use of gaze is a very important part of regulating face-to-face communication in difficult situations for a police officer.

2   Kidwell reviewed real video from the television show *COPS* to study how police officers use gaze. *COPS* is a reality program that

(continued on next page)

records police officers as they interact with people. Kidwell analyzed a 55-second video to see how a police officer used gaze to calm a hysterical woman. Her grandson had been shot, so she was very upset and couldn't communicate.

3   Kidwell cites other studies (Argyle and Cook [1976] and Kendon [1967, 1990]), becasue they found that gaze is very important for knowing if a person is participating in a conversation. When people gaze at one another, they share communication. If one does not return the other's gaze, he/she makes it difficult to communicate, In fact, that person may be *refusing* to interact.

4   According to Kidwell, when the hysterical woman in *COPS* refuses to look at the police officer, the officer understands it as an important sign of problems with their communication. As a result, he tries to fix the problem. Kidwell describes many different ways that the officer tries to get the woman to gaze at him. First, he talks to her. Next, he moves his head in line with her eyes. Finally, he puts his hand on her chin and turns her face toward him. In this way, the police officer actually *requires* her gaze.

5   The woman is able to listen and follow the police officer's instructions only after he holds her gaze. Kidwell concludes that gaze is the most important method of regulating face-to-face interaction.

COMMENTS

6   **Posted by Akiko N., October 30, 10:55 p.m.**
In my culture, touching someone's face like that would make them very uncomfortable. They might even get more agitated and upset. Looking the woman straight in the eye is inappropriate, because her experience and feelings are personal!

7   **Posted by Robert B., November 2, 8:17 p.m.**
Yeah, that's a cultural difference. Actually, I read another interesting study about why people avert their gaze like the woman in the study. People look away when they have to think really hard about something. The research says that looking away helps people shut out everything else so they can think. I wonder if that's universal or also cultural.

8   **Posted by Sean F., November 3, 4:23 p.m.**
Did Kidwell really only study 55 seconds of videotape to decide that gaze is such an important thing in police work?

9   **Posted by Robert B., November 3, 6:13 p.m.**
No. Actually, she studied 35 hours of footage, but she studied the 55 seconds in detail . . .

Source: Doherty-Sneddon, G., et al. (2002). Development of gaze aversion as disengagement from visual information. *Developmental Psychology, 38,* 438–445.

2. Complete the main idea statements about the summary and the students' comments.

1. Mardi Kidwell's study shows that _____
_____

2. The method of Kidwell's study was analyzing _____
_____

3. Earlier studies showed that _____
_____

4. Kidwell found that when the woman refused to meet the officer's gaze, he
_____

5. The conclusion of Kidwell's study is that _____
_____

6. Akiko thinks that _____
_____

7. Robert (in response to Akiko) says that _____
_____

Focused Reading

1. Complete the statements with details from the website on pages 145–146.

feels uncomfortable	reality television program	the year 2006
many different ways	rules of gaze	when they need to think

1. Kidwell performed her study in _____.
2. *COPS* is a _____ that shows events that actually happened.
3. Kidwell found that the police officer tried _____ to get the woman to look at him.
4. Akiko _____ with the police officer's actions toward the woman.
5. Akiko suggests that _____ are different in different cultures.
6. Robert writes that people look away _____.

In academic settings, you will be expected to learn a lot of new vocabulary. You can infer a new word's meaning by looking at clues in the context (the words and sentences before and after the word). Look for these kinds of clues:

- Synonyms (words very close in meaning)

synonyms

Example She was <u>quiet</u> and *tranquil*.

- Antonyms and contrasts (words and ideas with opposite meanings)

antonyms

Example The woman was <u>very upset</u> earlier, but now she is *sedate*.

- Examples or explanations used with the word

Example <u>Eye contact, gestures, and smiling</u> are all examples of *kinesics*.

- Grammar (noun, verb, adjective, adverb, etc.)

new word, word form = adjective

Example His nonverbal signals seemed *aggressive*.

2. *Work in small groups. Infer the meaning of the words from the reading. Follow the steps to complete the chart.*

1. Scan the website on pages 145–146 for the words listed in the chart.

2. Look for clues about the word's meaning. Write them in the chart.

3. Write the type of each clue (explanation, example, synonym, antonym, contrast, grammar).

4. Write a definition for each word.

Word	Clue(s)	Type of Clue(s)	Definition
traumatic (paragraph 1)	*people hurt, upset car accidents "difficult" situations*	*explanation example synonym*	*very bad, upsetting*
hysterical (paragraphs 2, 4)			
refuse (paragraphs 3, 4)			

Word	Clue(s)	Type of Clue(s)	Definition
avert (paragraph 7)			
footage (paragraph 9)			

3. *Write two other new words from the website in the chart in Exercise 2. Infer their meanings from context. Then share them with the class.*

4. *You will do an experiment in which you break a well-known nonverbal communication rule. Follow the steps to do the experiment.*

Step 1: Review the lecture, group discussion, and readings from this unit. In your notebook, take notes on specific rules of nonverbal communication and examples of nonverbal signals mentioned in the lecture, the discussion, and the reading. Then write examples from your own knowledge and experience. Keep your notes. You will need them later.

> **Example**
>
> *Lecture: to speak → make eye contact, raise eyebrows.*

Step 2: Choose a rule to break from your notes or from one of these examples:
- Try to take a turn in a conversation, but keep your head down.
- Make a gesture that is inappropriate for a situation.
- Gaze at a stranger for a long time.

Step 3: Perform your experiment—break the rule. Take notes on how others respond.

Step 4: Report the results of your experiment to the class.

Checkpoint 2 PEARSON LONGMAN myacademicconnectionslab⚓

4

Building Academic Speaking Skills

In this section, you will practice preparing role plays. You will also practice using stress, intonation, and pauses to express meaning. Then you will use ideas and vocabulary from this unit to write and present a role play demonstrating the importance of nonverbal communication.

For online assignments, go to

myacademicconnectionslab

Before you Speak

Presenting a Role Play

In academic classes you may be asked to create and perform a role play (short drama) to demonstrate your understanding of concepts you learn. Use these techniques to help make your performance more effective:

- Memorize the content of your role play—do not read it.
- Make note of nonverbal signals to use throughout your performance.
- Practice several times.
- Face your audience.
- Use a loud voice so that everyone can hear you clearly.
- Pay attention to stress and intonation in your voice

1. *Work with a partner. Complete the dialogue based on the* COPS *video scene you read about on pages 145–146. Practice the dialogue with your partner, using the techniques in the skill box.*

Example

WOMAN: Oh, no! He was SHOT! Oh! . . .

POLICE OFFICER: Now calm down. I need you to . . .

WOMAN: Where are they taking him? I've got to . . .

2. *Perform the role play for another pair of students. As you watch your classmates' performance, make a note of one thing they did well and one thing they could have done better.*

Focused Speaking

1. *Read the article about proxemics, a form of nonverbal communication that studies personal space.*

PROXEMICS FOR BETTER COMMUNICATION

The distance people keep between themselves and others expresses their level of comfort together and the closeness of their relationship. As the diagram shows, intimate space—the zone very near the body—is usually for people with whom we have a very close relationship, such as romantic partners. On the other hand, space farther away from the body is used with people we do not know as well. This idea is generally universal, though the exact distances vary from culture to culture and person to person.

Even small movements in and out of these zones can have a great effect on making another person more or less comfortable. For this reason, paying careful attention to the general guidelines in the diagram and to the nonverbal cues you receive will improve your communication.

Zones of Proxemics

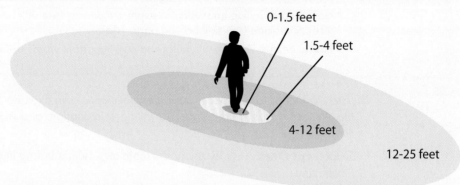

0-1.5 feet

1.5-4 feet

4-12 feet

12-25 feet

public space (12-25 feet): for presentations and public speaking
social space (4-12 feet): for most interaction at work, school, and with strangers
personal space (1.5-4 feet): for talking with family and friends
intimate space (0-1.5 feet): usually for very close relationships, but sometimes necessary in crowded places

Source: Based on Hall, E.T. (1966). *The hidden dimension.* Garden City, NY: Doubleday.

2. 🎧 *Listen to four short conversations. Mark the letter (A, B, C, or D) of the conversation next to the correct photograph. Then identify the zone shown in each photograph.*

1.

Conversation:_____

Zone: _____

2.

Conversation:_____

Zone: _____

3.

Conversation:_____

Zone: _____

4.

Conversation:_____

Zone: _____

In Unit 7, you learned to listen for stress and intonation in order to understand a speaker's meaning. When speaking, use these techniques to make your own ideas and feelings clear:

- **Stress** important words by saying them more loudly, slowly, and clearly.
- Use rising or falling **intonation** to express meaning (see skill box on page 128) or attitude (see skill box on page 143).
- **Pause,** or stop very briefly, before saying important words or ideas.

3. *Listen to individual sentences from the conversations in Exercise 2. Underline the stressed words, mark rising ↑ or falling ↓ intonation, and write a slash (/) to show pauses.*

🎧 **Excerpt One:** A really uncomfortable misunderstanding happened one day . . .

🎧 **Excerpt Two:** Well, guys, the project is due next Tuesday.

🎧 **Excerpt Three:** So, I can go to the library today to find some articles.

🎧 **Excerpt Four:** I'll go with you. Alberto, what can you do?

🎧 **Excerpt Five:** No! I'm just really upset right now . . .

🎧 **Excerpt Six:** I'll miss you too. I'll call you all the time.

4. *Work with a partner. Take turns repeating each statement in Exercise 3 as accurately as you can. Use your markings from Exercise 3 to help you remember the speakers' stress, intonation, and pauses.*

Integrated Speaking Task

You have read texts and listened to a lecture and a discussion about different types of nonverbal communication. You will now use your knowledge of the unit content, topic vocabulary, and inferences to write and present a role play in which you demonstrate nonverbal communication to imply ideas and feelings. You will also make inferences as you analyze the situations shown in your classmates' performances.

Follow the steps to prepare for your role play.

Step 1: Work in small groups to brainstorm ideas for a role play.

1. Compare your notes you made in Step 1 in Exercise 4 on page 149. Add examples related to proxemics.

2. Discuss the settings and situations in which the examples from your notes could cause clear communication or a misunderstanding. (For example, consider an interaction between people in a classroom, at a job interview, at a party, at a store, or at a police station.)

3. Decide together on a situation and some examples of nonverbal communication to show in your role play.

Step 2: Write your role play.

1. Outline the situation. Explain the cause(s) of understanding or misunderstanding. Include details about the specific nonverbal signal(s) used.

2. Write the dialogue, creating roles for every person in your group. Note the nonverbal cues that will be part of the communication. Mark the intonation, stress, and pauses you will use to imply ideas and feelings where possible.

Step 3: Review the techniques in the skill box on page 150, and practice your role play at least twice.

Step 4: Perform the role play for your class. Then give the audience two minutes to analyze the causes of understanding or misunderstanding, as well as your implied ideas and feelings.

For each role play you watch, take notes on these points to help you analyze the situation and inferences made:
- situation of role play
- nonverbal signals
- implied ideas and feelings
- result: clear communication or misunderstanding?

Step 5: As a class, discuss each role play and how it demonstrates the elements of nonverbal communication and inference skills you learned in this unit.

AUDIOSCRIPT

Psychology: First Impressions and Attraction

Global Listening

Exercise 1, Page 10

Professor: Hello everyone. Are we ready? OK . . . today I will talk about three elements of interpersonal attraction that are important in any relationship. If you remember, interpersonal attraction is when a person likes or wants a relationship with another person. When people hear this term, they think of romantic relationships. However, attraction is a part of *all* relationships, including those with friends, family, *and* romantic partners. So, the three elements I will talk about today are physical attractiveness, similarity, and exchange.

Lecture: Elements of Attraction

Professor: Hello everyone. Are we ready? OK . . . today I will talk about three elements of interpersonal attraction that are important in any relationship. If you remember, interpersonal attraction is when a person likes or wants a relationship with another person. When people hear this term, they think of romantic relationships. However, attraction is a part of *all* relationships, including those with friends, family, *and* romantic partners. So, the three elements I will talk about today are physical attractiveness, similarity, and exchange.

I'm sure it's not surprising that physical beauty is one of the most important elements of attraction. In his speed-dating study, Peter M. Todd found that the most important part of attraction for men was beauty, even if they said other qualities were more important. Other researchers have found that people believe that beautiful people are more intelligent, interesting, happy, and kind. Studies also show that teachers behave better toward attractive children, and mothers of beautiful babies give their babies more attention. Isn't that interesting?

Another important element of attraction is easy to understand: it is *similarity*. This means that two people feel that they are—more or less—the same. In a number of different studies psychologists found that people are more likely to choose friends and partners of the same age, race, class, and with similar opinions. This is because people who

are similar feel more confident around one another. They feel better about themselves. In Peter Todd's speed dating study, both men and women said that similarity was most important in choosing a partner.

The third element I want to talk about is *exchange*—this is when two people give to and receive from each other. For example, they can help each other, share things, and give love. The important point here is that people have to feel good about exchange in a relationship. Have you ever been in a relationship where one person gave more than the other? Was the relationship happy? Probably not. If two people feel good about their exchanges, they will continue in the relationship. And if not, the relationship can grow weak.

So in conclusion, there are three major elements of attraction that are important for all relationships: physical attractiveness, similarity, and exchange. Any questions?

Integrated Writing Task

Exercise 1, Page 16

Akiko: Excuse me. Do you know where the new student orientation is going to be?

Rosa: Yes. It's in room H305. My name's Rosa, by the way. What's yours?

Akiko: Oh, my name is Akiko. Thank you for your help, Rosa.

Rosa: Sure, Akiko. Akiko. . . that's a Japanese name, right? Are you from Japan?

Akiko: Yes, from Chiba.

Rosa: I'm from Mexico—Mexico City. How do you like it here?

Akiko: Um, it's OK. I just arrived last week, and it's my first time to travel alone.

Rosa: Oh! Are you by any chance Hiro's friend? He told me about a friend who was going to be a new student here. He said you're friendly, have short hair, and wear nice clothes. He was right! That bag is beautiful, by the way.

Akiko: Thank you. You know Hiro?

Rosa: Yes, we're good friends. I'm meeting him at the orientation because we are both student advisors and helping with the new students. We have an hour before orientation starts. Come on, I'll show you the cafeteria.

Akiko: OK. I'm very glad to meet you! Can I buy you a coffee to thank you for your help?

Rosa: That would be great. Thank you! ...Hiro told me you like to shop. I do too!

Akiko: Oh! I stepped on your foot. I'm so sorry.

Rosa: Don't worry. I didn't even notice.

UNIT 2

Ecology: The Web of Life

Lecture: Web of Life

Professor: Are we ready to begin? OK. . . Today, I'll continue on the topic of the web of life and discuss what happens when a part of the web is in danger. In particular, I'll discuss the ecosystem of the Amazon rain forest, and the effect of its destruction on life across the planet.

Like other ecosystems, all parts of the rain forest web of life are connected. Think about the Brazil nut tree: This tree depends on pollination by small bees and other insects for life. If this little piece of the tree's ecosystem was missing, the web would break, and there would be few Brazil nut trees. Consequently, people in the Amazon would lose an important food. This would also destroy an international business worth about $50 million a year.

Unfortunately, the web of life of the Amazon is in danger. In fact, 20 percent of the rain forest has disappeared, due to human actions. Local people and international companies are burning forests down to use the land for farms and farm animals. In addition, people around the world use paper and building materials made from millions of rainforest trees. These actions have serious effects on all living things.

First, because trees are disappearing, many animals are losing their homes and food. A lot of them die. Since many living things depend on each other, when some die, the whole web of life is affected.

The destruction of the rain forest also has serious consequences for people around the world. We use many trees and plants from the Amazon to produce medicines that help people with serious diseases. In fact, 70 percent of medicines for cancer come from rain forest plants. Aspirin and many other drugs you probably use come from rain forest plants, too. But scientists have tested only one percent of rain forest plants. Just one percent! Many unknown plants have also already disappeared, so scientists won't be able to study them and find more new medicines from them. This hurts all of us.

So, as you can see, destroying the rain forest has serious effects on living things across our planet. OK. . . next week, we're going to talk more about global warming. . .

Focused Listening
Exercise 2, Page 26

EXCERPT ONE
If this little piece of the tree's ecosystem was missing, the web would break, and there would be few Brazil nut trees. Consequently, people in the Amazon would lose an important food.

EXCERPT TWO
Many unknown plants have also already disappeared, so scientists won't be able to study them and find more new medicines from them.

EXCERPT THREE
Since many living things depend on each other, when some die, the whole web of life is affected.

Exercise 3, Page 26

Unfortunately, the web of life of the Amazon is in danger. In fact, 20 percent of the rain forest has disappeared, due to human actions. Local people and international companies are burning forests down to use the land for farms and farm animals. In addition, people around the world use paper and building materials made from millions of rain forest trees. These actions have serious effects on all living things.

First, because trees are disappearing, many animals are losing their homes and food. A lot of them die. Since many living things depend on each other, when some die, the whole web of life is affected.

Before You Speak
Exercise 1, Page 32

Student: My presentation today is on pollination, a very important ecosystem service. When we think about bees, usually the first thing we think of is sweet, delicious honey, right? Yeah, well—there is the surprising thing—beekeepers in the U.S. make more money today by *renting* honeybees to pollinate plants than by selling honey. Yeah. See, beekeepers put bees in boxes called beehives and take them all over the country to work on farms. But . . . now a *strange* thing is happening. Bees are leaving their beehives and not returning. One beekeeper in California lost 50 million bees in one day! Yeah. Really. Now, losing millions of bees is a real serious problem all over the world. Honeybee pollination services are worth $8.3 billion per year in the United States alone. If the bee population keeps growing smaller, there will be very costly consequences.

So, I know you're all asking, like, where did the bees go? What's happening? Right? Why are there fewer bees? Experts are studying this. Any guesses? First, just like all of us students, bees work too much and they have a poor diet—it's not natural. This can cause bees to get stressed and sick—just like with people. Finally, insecticides used on farms can hurt bees.

Like I said, there are serious consequences of losing bees. With no bees, *people* will have to pollinate all the foods that depend on insect pollination—including apples, onions, and about—oh—150 other fruits and vegetables. This would cause the food to be very expensive and not as good. So, in other words, losing bees is very costly for the economy. One expert says that losing bees may cause farmers in the United States to lose $15 billion—and other businesses to lose $75 billion.

In conclusion, bees are a super valuable part of our web of life. The effects of losing them can be very costly. Hopefully, we can find a way to save bees soon. OK. Are there any questions?

UNIT 3

Health: Stress and Health

Global Listening

Exercise 1, Page 49

Presenter: Hello everyone, and thank you to Dr. Ayala for inviting me to speak to your class today. Now. . . research shows that college students are more stressed now than in the past. Does that surprise you? So, today I'll talk to you about stress management techniques—helpful ways to manage or lower stress.

Lecture: Stress Management

Presenter: Hello everyone, and thank you to Dr. Ayala for inviting me to speak to your class today. Now. . . research shows that college students are more stressed now than in the past. Does that surprise you? So, today I'll talk to you about stress management techniques—helpful ways to manage or lower stress.

The first technique I want to talk about is called stress inoculation. When you use stress inoculation, you learn what gives you stress and then you try to change how you behave in that situation. For example, at least a few of you must be afraid of speaking in public. If you had to give a class presentation next week, you could prepare for this stressful event by taking small steps to get used to the situation. For instance, you could practice your presentation in front of your friends, in front of a mirror, or on video. Studies show this technique can reduce your anxiety in stressful situations.

Second, time management is an important way to lower stress. One of the things that causes students stress is feeling like there is too much to do. Studies like the ones by Campbell and Svenson in the 1990s show that good time management skills help students do better in school. One example of how you can manage your time is to make a schedule and write down what you do in a day—and how much time you spend on everything. This shows how you're using your time. Ask yourself questions like: Do I want or need to do each of these things, and for this long? If not, make changes. For example, you may need to spend less time in front of the TV. Another example of time management is making a list of things you need to do each day. You may realize that you need to divide projects into smaller steps so you can finish them. And that brings us to a surprising point: People who manage their time well, often schedule time to relax, too. That's also an important technique to use.

Finally, having a healthy lifestyle also helps manage stress. Things like exercising, eating good foods, and getting enough sleep keep your body strong and give you energy. When you feel healthy, you'll be able to manage stress better.

So to sum up, a few easy stress management techniques can help students in a lot of ways. They lower stress, help you live a healthier life, and help you be better students. Any questions?

Focused Listening

Exercise 3, Page 52

EXCERPT ONE
For example, at least a few of you must be afraid of speaking in public.

EXCERPT TWO
And that brings us to a surprising point: People who manage their time well often schedule time to relax, too.

EXCERPT THREE
Things like exercising, eating good foods, and getting enough sleep keep your body strong and give you energy. When you feel healthy, you'll be able to manage stress better.

UNIT 4

Literature: Folktales

Lecture: Common Characteristics of Folktales

Professor: Hi class. Good morning. Everyone ready? OK. For today's lecture we're going to talk about some common characteristics of the folktale. Most of us know some very old folktales. People shared these stories orally for years before writing them down. Since people told stories instead of writing them, the stories changed in between places and with each storyteller. Each new storyteller made changes to the stories based on his own traditions and culture. For example, many cultures have stories like the raven tale about how people got light. In these tales, though, the main character is another type of animal. So, to sum up, folktales began in the oral tradition, and as a result they have changed over time.

Next, the characters in folktales are similar. They are usually ordinary characters who do extraordinary things. They usually have only one or two strong characteristics. For instance, the chief in the Raven story is selfish and not very smart. But Raven is very generous—he wants to help people. And he's very clever as he finds a way to get the light. In addition, often the characters in folktales are not people but animals with human qualities. They talk, make plans, and have strong emotions. Small animals such as the popular spider and turtle play this role in West African stories. In summary, the characters of folktales are simple but often clever in achieving their goals.

Finally, the plot, or what happens in the folktale, is usually exciting. Most folktales begin with an expression like "a long time ago" and then move very quickly into the story, which starts with a problem. For instance, a strong, bad character often gives a weaker character a task and promises something if he completes the task. The weaker character often uses clever tricks, special skills, or magic to complete the task. In the end of a folktale, the good characters usually win and the bad characters lose. In conclusion, the plot of a folktale is interesting.

So, in summary, we know that the tradition of folktales is very old. They are told all over the world, but they share several of the same features—they began in the oral tradition and changed through the years, they also have the same types of characters and a strong plot.

Global Listening
Exercise 3, Page 64

So, in summary, we know that the tradition of folktales is very old. They are told all over the world, but they share several of the same features—they began in the oral tradition and changed through the years, they also have the same types of characters and a strong plot.

UNIT 5

Chemistry: Green Chemistry

Global Listening
Exercise 1, Page 90

Professor: Good morning, everyone. As you know, we have been talking about biofuels as an alternative to petroleum fuel. Today we will hear from Dr. Steven Schultz about a new kind of biofuel that has green chemists feeling excited. Dr. Schultz is a green chemist who works with governments and businesses on how they can benefit from alternative fuels. Please welcome Dr. Schultz.

Dr. Schultz: Well, thank you, Dr. Kim. You may think that chemists don't get excited, but we do. Sometimes we get really excited, and this is one of those times. We may have actually found a product—waste vegetable oil (also known as WVO)—that can solve some of our fuel problems. And, the great thing is, it already exists! Waste vegetable oil is oil that restaurants have used to cook food—like French fries. Then we process the oil into fuel for cars. So actually, this oil is used twice. Now, I know this may sound strange to a lot of you, but WVO is a good alternative when you think about it, because it's available, inexpensive, and as easy to use as, regular fuel.

Lecture: From French Fries to Fuel

Professor: Good morning, everyone. As you know, we have been talking about biofuels as an alternative to petroleum fuel. Today we will hear from Dr. Steven Schultz about a new kind of biofuel that has green chemists feeling excited. Dr. Schultz is a green chemist who works with governments and businesses on how they can benefit from alternative fuels. Please welcome Dr. Schultz.

Dr. Schultz: Well, thank you, Dr. Kim. You may think that chemists don't get excited, but we do. Sometimes we get really excited, and this is one of those times. We may have actually found a product—waste vegetable oil (also known as WVO)—that can solve some of our fuel problems. And, the great thing is, it already exists! Waste vegetable oil is oil that restaurants have used to cook food—like French fries. Then we process the oil into fuel for cars. So actually, this oil is used twice. Now, I know this may sound strange to a lot of you, but WVO is a good alternative when you think about it, because it's available, inexpensive, and as easy to use as regular fuel.

So, first of all, WVO is already available. For example, the U.S. produced over 11 billion liters of WVO in 2000. Don't you think that says a lot about our diet? Of course, all that oil from fried food has to go somewhere, right? It's usually just waste. So, using vegetable oil for fuel turns an existing waste into a valuable product. . . it's like turning garbage into gold! Right now restaurants have to pay to dispose of their cooking oil. So they are, of course, happy to give it away for free.

This brings me to another point—waste vegetable oil is quite cheap. . . definitely cheaper than petroleum prices now. When I work with companies and communities, we look at finding ways to use WVO because it's such a great deal—not only for people but for the environment.

Finally, WVO is easy to use. Actually, any car that runs on regular diesel can use vegetable oil. There are several ways to make it work. You can mix WVO with regular fuel and put it in the car. Or you can put a special part in your car to make it run on WVO.

So as you can see, waste vegetable oil is a simple and green alternative to petroleum that is available, cheap, and easy to use. Now, I'd be happy to answer any questions…

Focused Listening

Exercise 2, Page 91

EXCERPT ONE
You may think that chemists don't get excited, but we do.

EXCERPT TWO
For example, the U.S. produced over 11 billion liters of WVO in 2000. Don't you think that says a lot about our diet?

Exercise 3, Page 92

RADIO REPORT: DRIVING ON VEGETABLE OIL

Kent Glass (reporter): Waste vegetable oil is a great alternative for people like Peter Berger. The oil he uses is restaurant waste and was going to be thrown out anyway. So he can drive his car without feeling bad about polluting the environment.

Peter Berger (WVO user): When I need more oil, I simply go to the local Chinese restaurant or fast food restaurant. They are happy to give it away, and it doesn't cost me anything.

There *is* some difficulty with the process of cleaning oil so I can use it. And I had to get a new part put in my car, too. But it's worth the work.

Kim Wei (environmental studies expert): Yes, waste vegetable oil is a good alternative to petroleum fuel. . . But we also have to remember that there might be problems with producing vegetable oil just to drive cars. Already in the Amazon, people cut huge areas of forests so they can grow plants to produce vegetable oil for fuels. As a result, many animals and plants die. It also increases pollution and causes prices of food to rise. So, it really isn't the safest alternative.

UNIT 6

Art History: The Art of Marc Chagall

Global Listening

Exercise 1, Page 109

Professor: Good morning everyone. Now, you've been learning about Marc Chagall's life and themes in his art. Today we will talk more specifically about Chagall's independent style and what some critics think of his work.

Lecture: Chagall: Style and Criticism

Professor: Good morning everyone. Now, you've been learning about Marc Chagall's life and themes in his art. Today we will talk more specifically about Chagall's independent style and what some critics think of his work.

As you know, many painters of Chagall's time used abstract styles to show modern life and experiences such as war and difficult economic times. These artists believed that the old ways of painting could not show these experiences. Common themes in modernist art were social problems and loss of hope. On the other hand, with themes such as love, simple life, and nature, Chagall's art is easy to understand and full of hope. According to Jean-Michel Foray of the Chagall Museum, Chagall wanted people to understand what he was saying in his art. But some critics say that Chagall is just too simple and sentimental, a point I will return to later.

OK, so by now you probably realize that Chagall did not use just one technique. He used elements of many different styles in his work. In *I and the Village*, he used some cubist and modernist techniques: geometric shapes like circles and squares, bright colors, and showing objects in an unreal way. But at the same time, many of his subjects look real. This all creates a feeling of fantasy, doesn't it? His paintings are dreamlike. Look at the painting *The Birthday*. It shows a man and a woman. We know how much he loved Bella, so the man must be Marc and the woman must be Bella. Only one of the woman's feet is touching the ground, and both of Chagall's feet are off the ground, with his head turned to kiss her. And where are they? We see a bed and a dresser, so they may be in a bedroom. Maybe it's a dream? This is something we see so much of in Chagall: bringing together the real and the unreal. This might be what creates that feeling of dreamy joy.

Some art critics, however, criticize Chagall's work as being too sentimental. Sabina Ott of the San Francisco Art Institute says that Chagall's colors, for instance, are fantastic, but his simple subjects—flying animals and dreamy lovers—make his art too sentimental. Ott feels it doesn't make her look for a deeper meaning.

But Chagall's art might have a very important purpose. Art director Tim Riley explains how Chagall lived through two terrible world wars, but he always stayed interested in, quote, "the power of good in the world," because he believed art, quote, "could and should make the world a better place through themes of love and hope."

So in a time when many artists and thinkers lost hope, Chagall's work showed joy and beauty, and this made him unpopular with some critics. But why is Chagall's art so popular then? In my opinion, it must be because it shows what everyone wants to experience: love and hope. So what do you think?

Exercise 3, Page 110

EXCERPT ONE
Look at the painting *The Birthday*. It shows a man and a woman. We know how much he loved Bella, so the man must be Marc and the woman must be Bella.

EXCERPT TWO
Only one of the woman's feet is touching the ground, and both of Chagall's feet are off the ground, with his head turned to kiss her.

EXCERPT THREE
And where are they? We see a bed and a dresser, so they may be in a bedroom. Maybe it's a dream? This is something we see so much of in Chagall: bringing together the real and the unreal. This might be what creates that feeling of dreamy joy.

Focused Speaking

Exercise 1, Page 114

Roberto: So what do you see in Popova's *Lady with the Guitar*?

Claudia: Well, the painting is called *Lady with the Guitar*, so this must be the lady and that must be the guitar. But don't you think that the woman looks more like a man?

Roberto: I think so, too. That could be some writing on the left.

Claudia: I think you're right.

Roberto: And there's a table. It might be at a restaurant.

Claudia: I disagree with you. I don't see a table.

Roberto: Doesn't that square on the left right above the guitar look like a table?

Claudia: It looks like another square to me.

Roberto: Oh well. It looks like the person is wearing a dark shirt or suit.

Claudia: I agree. I can't tell if the person is alone or if there's an audience.

Roberto: Yeah, it's hard to tell. To me it looks like the person's alone.

Claudia: OK. So what do you think is the purpose of the painting?

Roberto: I believe that this painting shows a strong emotion: a deep feeling of sadness. The colors are all so dark.

Claudia: I agree, but I also think that the painting might be telling the story of a lonely guitar player who lost someone special. That's why the person is so sad and wearing black.

Roberto: I don't quite agree. But our time is almost up, so what about the style? Isn't the painting cubist? There are a lot of shapes like circles and squares.

Claudia: That's right. It really looks like a lot of cutout shapes. It reminds me a lot of Picasso's painting *The Guitar Player*. It's also very abstract like this one, and I know Popova was very influenced by Picasso's modernist ideas.

Roberto: I feel the same way.

UNIT 7

Marketing: Niche Marketing

Previewing the Academic Skills Focus
Exercise 2, Page 120

Lucy: I noticed Starbucks mentioned in the next homework assignment. I love Starbucks. What do they have to do with target marketing?

Professor: Actually, Starbucks is an interesting example of target marketing. Instead of focusing on fast and cheap coffee—like at fast food restaurants, for instance—Starbucks started with a plan to create a unique, European coffee experience. They wanted to serve high quality coffee drinks in a comfortable place where people could relax, think, and talk with others. So they targeted a very specific group of people: college-educated men and women between 18 and 30 that care about social issues like the environment.

Lucy: The same kind of customers they still target today?

Anthony: No, I don't think that they still target a niche market. You see everyone at Starbucks now: students, business people, families, children . . .

Professor: That's right, Anthony. As Starbucks has grown over the years, it's added other products and services to attract a larger market.

Exercise 3, Page 120

EXCERPT ONE
What do they have to do with target marketing?

EXCERPT TWO
Instead of focusing on fast and cheap coffee—like at fast food restaurants, for instance . . .

EXCERPT THREE
No, I don't think that they still target a niche market.

EXCERPT FOUR
That's right, Anthony.

Lecture and Role Play: The Power of Niche Markets

Teaching Assistant: Morning, class. OK, for today everybody read about niche marketing. Let's see. . . who can review the definition of a niche market for us? OK? How about you, Paul?

Paul: OK, uh, a niche market is a small, specific group of possible buyers who has a *real* need or want for a product or service.

TA: Yes, that's exactly right. Niche marketing means specializing in one small part of the market that most competitors don't serve. Maybe the market is too small for a big company to make enough of a profit, *or* maybe other companies have not identified the market's need for a certain product or service. OK, now, when you're out in the *real* world, let's say consulting with clients, you'll quickly realize that many small businesses want to serve everyone, even with a limited amount of money for marketing. This is not a good idea for a small business. It costs too much and makes it difficult to focus on the needs of customers.

So, let's do a role play to look at how you might help someone see the benefits of niche marketing. Imagine that I'm planning to start my own ice cream business. I need a team of consultants to help with my marketing plan. Any volunteers? Anyone at all? Don't all offer at once! OK, thank you, you, Nora and Park. Here we go! I'll start: "I need to find a lot of customers. If I limit my market to only *one* group of buyers, I won't make enough money. Plus, who doesn't like ice cream?"

Park: Well, how many millions of dollars do you *have* to market your product to the world? *You* can't do that. Instead of advertising to a large general market right away, you should become successful in a small niche first. If you don't, you will run out of money. There is too much competition in big markets.

TA: Well, I don't have a lot of money for marketing, but still, I'm *really* hoping to expand my business quickly.

Nora: But you won't make a profit that way. I guarantee you that your business will be stronger if you recognize who has the biggest need for your product and take time to understand that niche market. Then you can specialize to meet the *exact* needs of your customers. Plus, you'll be able to advertise more effectively, which saves money.

Park: Yeah. Take Jollibee, for instance. Even they started small by targeting a niche market.

Nora: Yeah, and once they became successful, they were able to expand and reach more customers. Now—in their market—they do better than *McDonalds*.

TA: Ah-ha. I see what you're saying. I need to think about who *really* wants my ice cream. Good job guys. Thanks for volunteering. Ok, moving . . .

Global Listening
Exercise 3, Page 127

EXCERPT ONE
Park: Instead of advertising to a large general market right away, you should become successful in a small niche first. If you don't, you will run out of money. There is too much competition in big markets.

TA: Well, I don't have a lot of money for marketing, but still, I'm *really* hoping to expand my business quickly.

EXCERPT TWO
Paul: OK, uh, a niche market is a small, specific group of possible buyers who has a *real* need or want for a product or service.

TA: Yes, that's exactly right. Niche marketing means specializing in one small part of the market that most competitors don't serve.

EXCERPT THREE
Nora: I guarantee you that your business will be stronger if you recognize who has the biggest need for your product and take time to understand that niche market. Then you can specialize to meet the *exact* needs of your customers. Plus, you'll be able to advertise more effectively, which saves money.

Park: Yeah. Take Jollibee, for instance. Even they started small by targeting a niche market.

Focused Listening
Exercise 3, Page 129

Well, how many millions of dollars do you *have* to market your product to the world? *You* can't do that.

UNIT 8

Communication: Nonverbal Communication

Previewing the Academic Skills Focus

Exercise 2, Page 140

I don't feel like my older brother listens to me, because of his nonverbal communication. He *tells* me he's listening, but I just don't believe it. Often when I'm talking, he doesn't even look at me, or he does something else. These signs tell me he's *not* listening. *He* needs to take this communication class.

Lecture and Discussion: Nonverbal Communication: Uses and Misunderstandings

Professor: Good morning! Let's get started. So, last time we talked about what nonverbal communication is. Let's review with an example. Have you ever wanted to say something in a conversation, but the other person just talked *on and on*? OK, so take a moment to imagine what you would do in this situation. Write down the nonverbal signals you might give to show you want to say something. Now, if you compared notes with the person next to you, would your signals be the same? That depends. See, everybody uses nonverbal communication, but the specific signals used are different among people and cultures. So today we're going to discuss two universal ways nonverbal communication is used, but also how people assume things based on personal interpretations.

Now, one way people use nonverbal communication is to regulate conversation, like in the example I just gave. In Western cultures when a listener wants a turn to speak to someone else, she will make eye contact with the speaker, or look straight in the speaker's eyes, and raise her eyebrows. In a large group, like in a classroom, a student will usually raise her hand to show she wants to speak.

In addition to helping to regulate a conversation, nonverbal signals can be used to quickly communicate an idea. When a specific body movement is used instead of words, it's called a *gesture*. Putting a finger to the lips can mean "be quiet," for example. Of course, you must be careful with gestures, because they're not the same across cultures. A gesture like putting your thumb up means "Good job!" in the United States, but it can easily get you in trouble in certain other cultures. Clearly, there is a lot of potential for misunderstanding with nonverbal signals.

Now, I'd like you to break into groups and discuss your own experiences with nonverbal communication . . .

Student 1: OK. . . The first point of the lecture was that people use nonverbal communication to regulate conversation. Anyone have an example of this?

Student 2: Yeah, like when I first left Japan and went to America, I had a *really* hard time talking in groups of Americans. They didn't give me a turn to speak. I was silent and polite—in the Japanese way—but they just talked and talked! It was difficult for me because they talked so much. It took me a long time to learn to give appropriate signals, but now I understand, and I am comfortable talking with Americans.

Student 3: I have an example of someone being rude. There's this guy in my math class—when the teacher asks a question, he doesn't just raise his hand to answer—he *waves it around*. Or, he calls out the answer. He just wants to make a good impression on the teacher, but the rest of us interpret this as inappropriate, because no one else has a chance to answer. It's good to raise your hand, of course—but *quietly*, ya know?

Global Listening

Exercise 3, Page 142

EXCERPT ONE
Of course, you must be careful with gestures, because they're not the same across cultures.

EXCERPT TWO
Yeah, like when I first left Japan and went to America, I had a *really* hard time talking in groups of Americans. They didn't give me a turn to speak. I was silent and polite—in the Japanese way—but they just talked and talked!

EXCERPT THREE
It took me a long time to learn to give appropriate signals, but now I understand and I am comfortable talking with Americans.

EXCERPT FOUR
I have an example of someone being rude. There's this guy in my math class—when the teacher asks a question, he doesn't just raise his hand to answer, he *waves it around*. Or, he calls out the answer.

Focused Listening

Exercise 3, Page 143

EXCERPT ONE
Like when I first left Japan and went to America, I had a *really* hard time talking in groups of Americans. . . . It was difficult for me because they talked so much.

EXCERPT TWO
But now I understand, and I am comfortable talking with Americans.

EXCERPT THREE

There's this guy in my math class—when the teacher asks a question, he doesn't just raise his hand to answer, he *waves it around*. Or, he calls out the answer.

EXCERPT FOUR

Of course, you must be careful with gestures, because they're not the same across cultures.

Focused Speaking

Exercise 2, Page 151

CONVERSATION A

Tom: Honey. Can't we talk about this? I'm so sorry.

Sonia: No! I'm just really upset right now. . .

CONVERSATION B

Sarah: I can't believe we graduated!

Ana: I'm really going to miss you guys.

Sarah: I'll miss you too. I'll call you all the time.

Jennifer: I know—and you'll text me all the time, too! Aw, I'm going to miss you so much. But we'll see each other during vacation too. . .

CONVERSATION C

Next, I'll tell you about another example of how nonverbal miscommunication affected my business trip overseas. A really uncomfortable misunderstanding happened one day…

CONVERSATION D

Eric: Well, guys, the project is due next Tuesday. So, I can go to the library today to find some articles.

Sue: I'll go with you. Alberto, what can you do?

Alberto: I'll look on the Internet.

Eric: OK, then let's meet again on Friday morning to put all the information together and plan our presentation.

CREDITS

Text credits: Page 2 (text and Exercise 2), "First Impressions and Hair Impressions: An Investigation of Impact of Hair Style on First Impressions," by Marianne LaFrance, February 2001.; **p. 3**, "At First Sight: Persistent Relational Effects of get-acquainted conversation," in *Journal of Social and Personal Relationships*, Vol. 21, by M. Sunnafrank and A. Ramirez, pp. 361-379.; **p. 13**, *Understanding Psychology*, 8th Edition by C. G. Morris and A. A. Maitson, 2008. Pearson Prentice Hall.; **p. 32**, "Estimating the Economic Value of Honey Bees as Agricultural Pollinators in the United States," in *Economic Entomology*, 85(3), by E. E. Southwick and L. Southwick, Jr., pp. 621 - 633. "Mystery Bee Disappearances Sweeping U.S.," by S. Lovgren, in *National Geographic News*, February 23, 2007.; **p. 39**, "The Social Readjustment Rating Scale," in *Journal of Psychosomatic Research*, 11, by T. Holmes and R. H. Rahe, 1967.; **pp. 42-43**, *Coping with Stress in a Changing World*, 3rd Edition, by R. Blonna, 2005. McGraw-Hill.; **p. 94**, "Plastic Bags, Sugar Cane and Advanced Vibrational Spectroscopy: Taking Green Chemistry to the Third World," in *Green Chemistry*, by M. Poliakoff and I. Noda, 2004, 6. Reprinted by permission of the Royal Society of Chemistry.; **pp. 101, 102**, "Celebrating Chagall," in *Online NewsHour*, by S. Michaels, 2003. Retrieved May 22, 2009 from http://www.pbs.org.; *March Chagall*, by F. Le Target, 1985. Rizzoli International Publications.; **pp. 122-123**, *Principles of Marketing*, 11th Edition, by P. Kotler and G. Armstrong, 2006. Pearson Prentice Hall.; **p. 133**, "Target a Niche Market to Increase Your Sales and Profits," by B. Leduc, 1999. Retrieved May 27, 2009 from http://www.soho.org/Marketing-Articles/Target-a-Niche.htm.; **p. 138**, *Silent Messages: Implicit Communication of Emotions and Attitudes*, by A. Mehrabian, 1981. Wadsworth.; **p. 146**, "Calm Down!: The Role of Gaze in the Interactional Management of Hysteria by the Police," in *Discourse Studies*, 8(6), by M. Kidwell, 2006.; **pp. 150-151**, *The Hidden Dimension*, by E. T. Hall, 1966. Doubleday.

Photo credits: Cover: Art on File/Corbis; **Page 1** (TR) Shutterstock, (T) Shutterstock, (M) Shutterstock, (B) Shutterstock; **p. 2** (T) Shutterstock, (MT) Dreamstime.com, (MB) Canstockphoto.com, (B) Shutterstock; **p. 4** Shutterstock; **p. 6** Shutterstock; **p. 9** Shutterstock; **p. 13** Shutterstock; **p. 16** Dreamstime.com; **p. 19** (TR) Shutterstock, (T) Shutterstock, (B) Dreamstime.com; **p. 20** (L) Dreamstime.com, (M) Photo courtesy of Gosia Jaros-White, (R) Shutterstock; **p. 24** Shutterstock; **p. 27** www.awag.org; **p. 29** Dorling Kindersley; **p. 31** Shutterstock; **p. 33** Shutterstock; **p. 37** (TR) Shutterstock, (T) Shutterstock, (B) Dex Images/Corbis; **p. 38** (L) Shutterstock, (T) Shutterstock, (R) Mark Wilson/Getty Images, (B) Radius Images/Alamy; **p. 42** (L) David Crausby/Alamy, (R) Dex Images/Corbis; **p. 49** (T) Shutterstock, (B) Shutterstock; **p. 56** Shutterstock; **p. 59** (TR) Shutterstock, (M) Spencer Grant/PhotoEdit; **p. 60** (T) Shutterstock; **p. 64** Spencer Grant/PhotoEdit; **p. 67** Shutterstock; **p. 79** (TR) Shutterstock, (background) Shutterstock, (T) Shutterstock, (M) Shutterstock, (B) Shutterstock; **p. 80** Shutterstock; **p. 85** Shutterstock; **p. 90** Shutterstock; **p. 94** Issouf Sanogo/AFP/Getty Images; **p. 96** Moodboard/Corbis; **p. 99** (TR) Shutterstock, (B) Digital Image © The Museum of Modern Art/Licensed by SCALA/Art Resource, NY ©2009 Artists Rights Society (ARS), New York/ADAGP, Paris; **p. 100** (L) Art Resource, NY, (M) Banque d'Images, ADAGP/Art Resource, NY ©2009 Artists Rights Society (ARS), New York/ADAGP, Paris, (R) Francis G. Mayer/Corbis; **p. 101** (L) Museum of Art, Smolensk, Russia/SuperStock, (R) Digital Image © The Museum of Modern Art/Licensed by SCALA/Art Resource, NY ©2009 Artists Rights Society (ARS), New York/ADAGP, Paris; **p. 103** Li Erben/Kipa/Corbis; **p. 104** Digital Image © The Museum of Modern Art/Licensed by SCALA/Art Resource, NY ©2009 Artists Rights Society (ARS), New York/ADAGP, Paris; **p. 108** Jaubert Bernard/Alamy; **p. 109** Digital Image © The Museum of Modern Art/Licensed by SCALA/Art Resource, NY ©2009 Artists Rights Society (ARS), New York/ADAGP, Paris; **p. 114** Museum of Art, Smolensk, Russia/SuperStock; **p. 115** Banque d'Images, ADAGP/Art Resource, NY ©2009 Artists Rights Society (ARS), New York/ADAGP, Paris; **p. 117** (TR) Shutterstock, (M) Jeff Greenberg/PhotoEdit; **p. 118** (L) Business Wire/Getty Images, (R) Dreamstime.com; **p. 120** (L) Jay Directo/AFP/Getty Images, (R) Jay Directo/AFP/Getty Images; **p. 122** Romeo Gacad/AFP/Getty Images; **p. 125** Jay Directo/AFP/Getty Images; **p. 127** Jeff Greenberg/PhotoEdit; **p. 130** (T) Shutterstock, (B) Shutterstock; **p. 131** Canstockphoto.com; **p. 137** (TR) Shutterstock, (T) Dreamstime.com, (M) Shutterstock, (B) Image Source/Corbis; **p. 139** Radius Images/Jupiterimages; **p. 140** www.CartoonStock.com; **p. 141** Dreamstime.com; **p. 145** Kayte M. Deioma/PhotoEdit; **p. 151** (TL) Shutterstock, (TR) Shutterstock, (BL) Image Source/Corbis, (BR) Jupiterimages/Comstock Images/Alamy.

Illustration credits: Paul Hampson, **Page 81**; Brian Hughes, **Pages 84, 89**; Gary Torrisi, **Pages 20, 22, 68, 75**

AUDIO CD TRACKING GUIDE

(continued on next page)